The Second Tang Dynasty

The 12 sons of Fragrant Mountain who changed China

MARK O'NEILL

Contents

Preface

It is Sunday lunchtime in a noisy Hong Kong restaurant. My mother-in-law is describing the war years in her native place (or township) Tangjiawan, part of Zhuhai in Guangdong province. "The 'carrot heads' (Japanese soldiers) used to take a shower every afternoon in the open air. We children used to peep around the wall to watch them. They did not look so menacing in the nude." She thinks for a moment: "We had important neighbours, you know. The house of Tang Shao-yi is next to ours. He was one of many important people from Tangjiawan. As children, we used to play in his enormous garden, with trees, hills and a pool. There was nowhere like it in the village."

I was too embarrassed to admit that, despite living in China for many years, I had never heard of Tang Shao-yi. When I got home, I checked on the Internet and found that he was the first Prime Minister of the Republic of China, a distinguished diplomat and later chief of his native county. He bequeathed his private domain to the township after his death in 1938 – the reason why Mother-in-law was able to play there. I was ashamed of my ignorance.

After more research, I discovered that she had not been exaggerating when she talked about the famous sons of Tangjiawan – a township comprising several villages and part of what was then called Xiangshan county (now known as Zhongshan). This small county in a remote corner of China, far from the Imperial court in Beijing and the commercial metropolis of Shanghai, produced the man who took the first 120 Chinese children to study in the United States, the first Chinese doctor of western medicine, the first president of Tsinghua University, one of the first admirals of the Chinese navy, the founders of the country's modern retail industry and several of the most important business leaders of the late Qing and early Republican periods.

I thank Mother-in-law for providing the idea of this book. I picked 12 of the most prominent sons of Xiangshan and asked: how could a small county with a population of only several thousand in 1880 produce such remarkable individuals who left a great mark on China? What were the social and historical events that caused this to happen? How did these individuals move from a backward rural society into the ministries, the banking halls and university campuses of Beijing and Shanghai? What personal challenges did they have to overcome on the way?

Like many of its residents, Mother-in-law left Tangjiawan in 1949 with her mother and one of her two brothers, after the arrival of the new government, and came to Hong Kong. The frontier was closed and she could not return; but she never forgot the friends and classmates she had left behind and stayed in touch as best she could. In August 1980, Deng Xiao-ping（鄧小平）declared Zhuhai – which was part of Xiangshan county and now includes Tangjiawan – a Special Economic Zone (SEZ). In 1985, with members of the family for company, she made her first visit back since 1949. It was a shock. Most of the residents did not speak Cantonese, but Mandarin; they were migrants from Sichuan, Jiangxi and other provinces attracted by new opportunities in the SEZ. This large influx had greatly changed the physical appearance of the township; new homes and shops filled land that had been rice paddies and football fields. After this initial discomfort, however, Mother-in-law began to feel more at home.

She met former school classmates; they started to talk in the Cantonese dialect used in the township. We found the house where she was born and grew up; it was unchanged, with a courtyard and high ceiling that creates a flow of air as well as a fan. She took off down the narrow alley to the house where Tang Shao-yi was born. A five-minute walk away was Tang's garden where she had played with the other children. Now called the "Park of Public Happiness" (Gong Le Yuan, 共樂園), it was the same as when she played there: a sprawling domain full of trees, small hills, traditional pavilions, a lake and the houses in which Tang had lived with his family. One of them has been turned into a museum of his life.

The photographs conveyed his extraordinary history – standing with Dr. Sun Yat-sen（孫逸仙）on his first day as Prime Minister in March 1912, meeting American friends like Presidents Theodore Roosevelt and Herbert Hoover and entertaining the artistic and political elite of China at his Tangjiawan home.

Mother-in-law also took us to an ageing cinema and cultural centre; in the hall at the front were photographs of the famous sons of the township she had talked about. For the first time, I could put faces to the names I had heard. They were proud and self-confident, men who had achieved something in their lives; they had the smooth skin of someone who works indoors, not the faces of a farmer or fisherman. Many were called "Tang", the same as Mother-in-law; Tangjiawan means "the bay of the Tang family".

I looked up the life of Tang Shao-yi. In 1874, at the age of 12, he was one of 40 students to go to the United States. He stayed with a family in Springfield, Massachusetts, graduated with honours from a high school at Hartford, Connecticut and enrolled at Columbia University in New York. He was only able to complete one year before he and the other students were recalled by the government; it was afraid they were becoming westernized and losing their "Chineseness".

His seven years in the U.S. gave Tang a competitive edge when he returned home; he could speak fluent English and had a knowledge and experience of the western world rare among his countrymen. It was the 1880s: China was under assault by the colonial powers and their companies eager to exploit its rich resources and products. The Qing government was hopelessly ill-equipped to resist. A person like Tang was invaluable to the government; he was sent to Korea, the start of a distinguished diplomat career.

I discovered that this exposure to the outside world was the secret of success of the famous sons of Xiangshan. Each had left their home village, some going to Macao and Hong Kong and others to the U.S., Britain, Australia and Japan. In these foreign lands, they, like Tang, acquired skills and knowledge that they brought home. Some went into public service, others worked for themselves; they had drive, ambition and determination to achieve something in their lives. All made an important contribution to China in their respective fields, helping an inward-looking feudal kingdom to become a modern state.

In the title, we use Xiangshan (Fragrant Mountain, 香山), the name for the county to which Tangjiawan belongs. After the death of Sun Yat-sen (Sun Zhong-shan, 孫中山), its most famous son, in 1925, the name was changed to Zhongshan (中山) county in his honour; it still uses that name today.

Let us begin with Rong Hong, Yung Wing in Cantonese. He was the pioneer, one of the first Chinese to study in the United States and the first to graduate from Yale University. It was he who devised the plan to send Chinese students to the U.S. and follow his footsteps; 120 of them did so, including Tang Shao-yi. He was the founder of what became a virtual second Tang dynasty of influential men from Xiangshan.

The author would like to thank the Macao Foundation for its support for this book. It greatly facilitated the research and the writing.

Chapter One

The Pathfinder

容閎
1828 - 1912

Yung Wing

Introduction

Yung Wing was one of the most remarkable Chinese of the 19th century. Born into a poor farming family in Xiangshan county in Guangdong, he had the great good fortune to receive a western education in Macao, Hong Kong and the United States.

Considered the Chinese Columbus who "discovered' America", Yung was the first Chinese graduate of Yale University.

He could have enjoyed a comfortable and prosperous life in the U.S. but, instead, he chose to return home to dedicate himself to the reform and modernization of China. As the country had an imperial government that was arrogant and xenophobic this was an enormous challenge.

Yung went to the U.S. to purchase machinery for the Jiangnan shipyard in Shanghai, where China was for the first time able to manufacture the same type of heavy weapons used by the western powers.

In 1870, the government accepted his plan to send young Chinese to the U.S. to follow his example and learn science, technology and the secrets of the modern world. It appointed him to organize the programme. Between 1872 and 1881, he was responsible for 120 students sent to America for education in secondary schools and universities – before the project was cancelled by conservatives within the Qing government.

After their return, these students made an enormous contribution to the modernization of China, in education, engineering, diplomacy, medicine, industry, the military, business and other fields. They were the pioneers. Over the last 30 years, hundreds of thousands of Chinese have followed their footsteps and studied in universities in North America, Europe and Japan, bringing home the skills and knowledge they have acquired.

Yung was a strong supporter of Emperor Guangxu (光緒) and had to flee for his life to Hong Kong after the failure of his reforms in 1898. He supported the revolutionary programme of Dr. Sun Yat-sen and learnt of the success of the Xinhai Revolution in October 1911 while at his home in Hartford, Connecticut. Sun invited him to return to China but he died in Hartford on April 21, 1912.

In 1876, at its centennial commencement, Yale University awarded him an honorary Doctor of Law for his enormous contributions to cultural exchanges between China and the U.S. In 2004, it erected a statue in his honour, on the 150th anniversary of his graduation.

Childhood

Yung was born on November 17, 1828 in Nan Ping village, on Pedro Island six kilometres southwest of Macao.

The third of four children, he had an elder brother and sister and a younger brother. It was a poor family; his father rented three mu (0.2 hectares) of land and raised fish and shrimp. Nan Ping had no school; his father sent his elder brother to a private school in a nearby village.

By chance, a neighbour and friend of his father was the principal servant in the Macao home of Mrs Mary Wanstall Gutzlaff, the wife of Rev Karl Gutzlaff, a Protestant missionary; the couple had set up a school for Chinese children. This neighbour informed his father about the school; thanks to this introduction, the young boy was admitted in 1835, at the age of seven.

"It has always been a mystery to me why my parents should take it into their heads to put me into a foreign school, instead of a regular orthodox Confucian school, where my elder brother was placed," wrote Yung in his autobiography *My Life in China and America*, published in 1909.

Going to a Confucian school "would have been more in play with Chinese public sentiment, taste and the wants of the country at large than to allow me to attend an English school." A Chinese school was the only avenue to professional advancement, power and wealth.

"As foreign intercourse with China was just beginning to grow, my parents, anticipating that it might soon assume the proportions of a tidal wave, thought it worthwhile to take time by the forelock and put one of their sons to learning English so that he might become one of the advanced interpreters and have a more advantageous position from which to make his way into the business and diplomatic world," he wrote.

As a resident of Xiangshan, Yung's father had a broader perspective than most Chinese; since the arrival of the Portuguese in Macao nearly 300 years before, Xiangshan had been greatly influenced by this western trading and religious centre. Many of its people had gone to work and settle there and prospered. Yung's father saw the benefits of an education that would enable his son to work in both the western and Chinese worlds.

Another reason was that tuition and boarding at the Macao school were free, while Chinese schools charged fees.

All the same, it was a brave decision by a farmer in rural China to do something so unusual; he was not sending his son to a famous and well-established school but one that had just been set up by a couple and would have been illegal in mainland China.

Macao School

The school was established by British missionary teacher Mary Wanstall who had gone to Malacca to teach; there she met Prussian missionary Karl Gutzlaff; they moved to Macao in December 1831 and married in 1834.

They decided to use their house as a school to provide a western Christian education for Chinese children; she was the teacher and principal. It was the first school of this kind in China. The funding came from the Morrison Education Society (MES), set up in memory of Robert Morrison, the first Protestant missionary in China who died in Guangzhou on August 1, 1834, aged 52, and is buried in the Protestant cemetery of Macao.

This society was established by wealthy British and American merchants; they admired this pioneer who had translated the Bible into Chinese and wrote the first English dictionary of the Chinese language in six volumes. They wanted to continue his work of education through the society. Its mission was "to improve and promote English education in China by schools and other means."

The Protestant church of Macao, near Camoes Garden, is also named after Robert Morrison; the land for the chapel and the adjoining cemetery was purchased in 1821, following the death of Mary, Morrison's wife.

The school was close to the ruins of St. Paul's church, which had been devastated by a terrible fire on January 26, 1835.

The MES provided 15 pounds a month to the Gutzlaffs to run their school. It opened on September 30, 1835, with 12 girls and two boys, of whom Yung was one. Additional funding came from the Ladies Association for the Promotion of Female Education.

Since her husband was away most of the time, distributing religious tracts along the China cost, it was Mary Gutzlaff who fed, clothed and educated the pupils. They had lessons in both English and Chinese.

When Yung was seven years old, his father took him to start his new life at the school, where he would be a boarder. They left Nan Ping village and made the crossing to Macao in a small boat.

They walked to the school and the boy met Mrs Gutzlaff. He had never in his life set eyes on a "Big Nose", let alone one in a long, flowing white dress; trembling, he clung to his father in fear.

"She was somewhat tall and well-built," he wrote. "She had prominent features which were strong and assertive; her eyes were of clear blue lustre, somewhat deep set. She had flaxen hair and eyebrows somewhat heavy. Her features taken collectively indicated great determination and will power ... I was less puzzled than stunned – having never in my life seen such a peculiar and odd fashion."

Fortunately, she was able to win him over through her kindness and sympathy. Since he was the youngest student in the school, she kept a particular eye on him and lodged him among the girl students on the third floor of the school, while the other boy was on the ground floor.

Yung adjusted quickly to his new environment and came to like his teacher. But he resented being confined to the school; he and the girls were not permitted to go outside.

So, one day during the first year, he organized an escape with six of the girl students. While Mrs Gutzlaff was having breakfast, they ran to a nearby wharf where they had hired a boat, with two oars, to take them the short distance to Pedro Island where his family lived.

But they were not quick enough. Madame organized a search party, a boat with four oars which overtook them; the seven were brought back to the school in disgrace and forced to stand for an hour in front of the other pupils. On Yung's chest was a placard with the words "Head of the Runaways"; he stood in the middle of the six girls. "I never felt so humiliated in my life."

He did not make this mistake again; he devoted himself to study, learning English and other subjects taught in a western school; this put him among the tiny fraction of the 413 million subjects of the Qing emperor who had such knowledge.

In 1839, as relations between Britain and China deteriorated over the issue of opium and war seemed likely, Mary Gutzlaff decided to leave Macao for reasons of personal safety and go to the U.S.; she took with her three blind girls whom she was teaching at the school.

As a result, her school closed; together with the other students, Yung went home. He went to work, selling candy in his home village and a neighbouring one; he rose at 3a.m. and did not come home until 6p.m., earning 25 cents a day which he gave to his mother. In spring, he went to work in the rice paddies.

In the autumn of 1840, Yung's father died, leaving his mother without her principal means of support and making it essential that her children worked to earn a living.

Later Yung went to work for a Catholic priest in Macao; the priest needed someone with sufficient English to do clerical work. Yung was paid a modest salary, of which he sent the lion's share to his mother. Then, for two months, he helped a foreign missionary doctor at his hospital in Macao, preparing materials for pills and ointments and accompanying him as he went round the wards.

Morrison School

Meantime, the MES wanted to set up a larger school for boys and began a search in Britain and the U.S. for a minister to run it.

They found the person in Reverend Samuel Robbins Brown, who was born in Connecticut on June 16, 1810 and graduated from Yale University; he would play a critical role in the life of Yung Wing.

Brown studied theology in Columbia, South Carolina and taught from 1834-1838 in the New York Institution for the Deaf and Dumb. Eager to become a missionary abroad, he applied for the post in Macao and was accepted. He and his wife arrived in Macao on February 24, 1839, having been given free passage on the boat from the U.S. because the owner wanted to help missionaries.

On November 4, 1839, he opened the school in a house provided by the MES, with five students. It taught primary arithmetic, geography and reading, using English in the morning and Chinese in the afternoon; each day they had eight hours of classes and three-four hours of exercise and recreation in the large grounds. They were not allowed to leave the premises. Each year they spent a month at home, during the Spring Festival.

"It is not merely a teaching but an education society," wrote Brown in a report to the MES trustees on April 29, 1840. "It aims at the training of the entire man, physical, intellectual and moral."

Yung had been out of school for a year but the directors of the MES remembered him as an excellent student and were keen to bring him back. In 1841, the doctor took Yung to the school, where he became the sixth student. The tuition and board of the students were paid by the society and private individuals.

In 1842, the school moved from Macao to Hong Kong, after the island was ceded to the British government as a result of the Opium War. The government donated the school a site 600 feet above sea level that is still known as "Morrison Hill".

Opium

Yung and his fellow students owed their education to the generosity of western missionaries and the business people who established and funded the MES. There were also in Macao missionary doctors, bringing to its people a quality of care they had never received before.

The missionaries believed they were bringing to Chinese the blessings of the civilization from which they came. In terms of medical care, education and religion, they were right.

But a terrible shadow hung over their work – the opium trade. Many of the merchants who established the MES worked for companies whose principal commodity was opium, grown in India and sold in China despite the repeated and impassioned orders of the government to end the trade.

William Jardine worked for 14 years with the East India Company before he established Jardine, Matheson and Company in 1832. Its main commodities were opium, tea, silk and cotton. It was he who in 1839 persuaded the British Foreign Secretary, Lord Palmerston, to wage war against China over the issue of opium; he provided him with a detailed plan, maps, strategies and even the number of troops and warships required. He was an original board member of MES and also contributed to the Macao Ophthalmic Hospital.

Lancelot Dent was also an original board member and donated to the hospital. With his brother, he set up Thomas Dent & Company, which was second in size to Jardine, Matheson; it was also active in opium. It was the warrant by Chinese commissioner Lin Zexu for the arrest of Dent in 1839, to force him to hand over his store of opium, that sparked the First Opium War.

In 1839, Lin destroyed 20,000 chests of opium in Guangzhou. Unwilling to replace opium with costly silver as the commodity to pay for Chinese goods, the British started the war in 1839.

Many Chinese associated evangelism with opium. The missionaries first came to China on the ships carrying it and travelled on them to reach ports along the Chinese coast. Robert Morrison worked in Guangzhou as translator for the East India Company, the main supplier of opium.

Karl Gutzlaff, the husband of Yung's first teacher, also used the opium ships to carry missionary tracts to different cities in China.

"Opium in one hand and the Bible in the other" was an accusation that would be made against the western missionaries for the next 100 years. During the second half of the 19th century, they would become one of the strongest opponents of the trade, especially the missionary doctors and ministers who saw the devastating effects of opium on the Chinese who were their patients and members of their congregation.

Yung and his classmates were the lucky ones. They received the best things the foreigners had to offer – and not the drug which ruined the lives of millions of their compatriots.

Going to America

Yung and his five classmates studied and lived peacefully in the Morrison school in its new location in Hong Kong, where the number of students grew to more than 40. It was a happy and harmonious environment; The Browns treated the students as members of their own family; the boys responded with their love and loyalty.

Then one day in August 1846 changed his life.

Out of the blue, Rev Brown told a school assembly that, because his own and his family's health was deteriorating, he had decided to return to the U.S.. "I have a great love and interest in the school and would like to take a few of its pupils with me to finish their education. Those who wish to go, please stand up."

Everyone was stunned by this news; they liked Brown very much and could not conceive of the school without him. Who could imagine crossing the ocean to go to a distant and mysterious country?

Several minutes passed; nobody moved. Then Yung stood up, followed by two others, Huang Kuan and Huang Sheng. Brown told the three to obtain the agreement of their parents to this drastic decision.

"My mother gave her consent with great reluctance," said Yung. "After my earnest persuasion, she yielded but not without tears and sorrow." He consoled her by saying that she had three other children to look after her, as well as a daughter-in-law since his elder brother was about to marry.

The three would be the first Chinese to go as students in the U.S.; it was a historic moment. It was made possible by the generosity of British and American patrons who wanted to help the three in their education; they also agreed to give financial support to their parents for two years.

In addition, David Olyphant and his two brothers, who owned a trading company named after them, provided free passage from Hong Kong to New York for the Browns and the boys on their ship "the

Huntress"; it was carrying a cargo of tea. Theirs was the only major trading company that refused to deal in opium; as a result, its offices were known as "Zion's corner". They wished to support the missionary project.

The vessel set out from Hong Kong on January 4, 1847 and went, via the Cape of Good Hope, to St. Helena, where they found a small number of Chinese families and visited the empty tomb of Napoleon Bonaparte. They arrived in New York harbour on April 12, 1847. It was a city of more than 400,000 people.

Rev Brown took the three boys to Monson, Massachusetts and placed them under the care of his mother Phoebe; she gave them a room in a house opposite her own. She looked after them, cooking meals for them every day.

The three went to study at the Monson Academy, a private prep school founded in 1804, one of the 15 oldest schools on the east coast of the U.S.. It was an elite academic school out of reach of the vast majority of Americans; it was an escalator into the ruling class of society, like the expensive private schools of Britain on which it was modelled.

Its principal was Reverend Charles Hammond, who was, like Brown, a graduate of Yale University. They wanted to send the three young Chinese there; Yale and Harvard were the two most famous universities in the country. Their courses included natural science, humanities, biology, literature, mathematics and philosophy.

In the autumn of 1848, Huang Sheng, the eldest of the three, decided to return to China because of his poor health; that left two behind. They graduated from Monson Academy in the summer of 1849, including 12 months of ancient Greek and 15 of Latin. Yung's best subject was English literature. He was weak in mathematics and had to work hard to pass the exam for Yale.

Their patrons in Hong Kong informed them that they were willing to support their further education if they went to the University of Edinburgh in Scotland. This Huang Kuan decided to do; he graduated from there as a doctor, the first Chinese graduate in western medicine, and returned to China in 1857. He went on to a distinguished career as a doctor and teacher (please read about his life in the next chapter).

Entering Yale

Yung wanted to stay in the U.S. and study at Yale. At the same time, he was under pressure from his family, and especially his mother, to return home and earn money to support them. They feared that he would become a devout Christian and never go back to China.

In his letters home, he stressed that he was only staying in the U.S. in order to complete his studies and would then return home. In the winter of 1850, his mother wrote to tell him that his younger brother had passed away. "This letter made me extremely sad for two weeks," he wrote to a friend in Guangdong. "In the eyes of my soul, I can see the difficulty they are in. I ought to go home but, given the situation as it is, I can only pray for them."

Despite these difficulties, he was successful in passing the exam to enter Yale University, the first Chinese to do this; it was an astonishing achievement for the son of a poor farmer from a Guangdong village.

But, since he did not have the necessary funds for tuition and board, he asked Rev Brown and Principal Hammond for advice.

They arranged for him to meet the trustees of a fund for poor students; they told him that they were willing to provide money on condition that, after graduation, he return to China and work as a missionary.

Yung thanked them for the offer, but declined. "I wanted the utmost freedom of action to avail myself of every opportunity to do the greatest good in China," he wrote. Second, he was not so devout a Christian. Third, such a pledge "would prevent me from taking advantage of any circumstance or event that might arise in the life of a nation like China, to do her a great service."

However, he obtained funding from The Ladies Association of Savannah, Georgia and the Olyphant brothers who had given him free passage on the boat from Guangzhou. In addition, he worked as a steward of a boarding club; he cleaned clothes, served at tables and bought provisions. He also worked as a librarian. From these sources, he received enough money to support him during his years of study.

Yung was the only Chinese in the student body. His strongest subject was English composition, for which he won two academic prizes – which was remarkable for a foreigner. He was also strong in metaphysics but weak in Greek and mathematics. Beyond the classroom he enjoyed physical exercise, especially the American brand of football, which he played with the pigtail of a Qing Chinese waving behind his head; it attracted the attention and amusement of his fellow students. Rounding out a very full list of extra-curricular activities, he was also a member of the university boat club and sang in the choir.

Yung became an American citizen in October 1852.

In 1854, he graduated in English literature in a class of 98 students, the first Chinese graduate of Yale University. Many came to the ceremony in order to see this Chinese graduate.

Rev Joseph Twitchell, who would become his brother-in-law, later described Yung's years at Yale, in an address to the Kent Club of its Law School on April 10, 1878. "His nationality made him a good deal of a stranger and this, together with his extreme natural reserve and his poverty, kept him from mingling much with the social life of college. He had not many inmates (close friends), yet he so carried himself from first to last as to merit and win the entire respect of all his class."

Return to China

During his final year, Yung thought deeply about his future and how to make use of this privilege of higher education he had received. He had developed a deep feeling for the U.S., becoming an American citizen, and regarded it as his second home; he had made many friends.

But his home country was foremost in his thoughts. His friends wrote to him about the Taiping Rebellion which had broken out in 1850. It was led by a Christian convert Hong Xiu-quan who believed that he was the younger brother of Jesus Christ.

At its height, Hong's army controlled large parts of southern China, with a population of more than 30 million people. During the rebellion, which was finally crushed in 1864, about 20 million people died, mainly civilians; it was one of the deadliest military conflicts in history.

"The lamentable condition of China was before my mind constantly and weighed on my spirits. Before the close of my last year in college, I had already sketched out what I should do. I was determined that the rising generation of China should enjoy the same educational advantages that I had enjoyed: that through western education China might be regenerated, become enlightened and powerful. To accomplish that object became the guiding star of my ambition. Toward such a goal, I directed all my mental resources and energy," he wrote.

With his diploma, his connections and his citizenship, he could have settled in the U.S. and enjoyed a comfortable and successful life. Companies and research organizations offered him a job; but he declined them. He does not even mention this possibility. His mother country was always in his thoughts. In returning, he knew that he would encounter suspicion and prejudice because of what he had become.

He did wish to stay a few years more to learn surveying. "But I was poor and my friends thought that a longer stay might keep me here for good and China would lose me altogether." So he determined to return.

On November 13, 1854, he left New York on the sailing clipper "Eureka" in the company of Rev William Allen Macy, who had replaced Rev Brown as the principal of the Morrison School in Hong Kong.

The journey of 13,000 nautical miles to Hong Kong lasted 154 days; he described it as the most uninteresting and wearisome voyage of his life. He and Macy were the only passengers; the ship was empty of cargo or ballast, with the result that it had little to protect itself from the fury of the waves.

On arrival in Hong Kong, he rushed to Macao to see his mother for the first time in 10 years. "We met with tears of joy, gratitude and thanksgiving. Our hearts were too full even to speak at first. She began to stroke me all over, as expressive of her maternal endearment which had been held in patient suspense for at least 10 years."

She asked how much money he received as a result of graduating from Yale. "Knowledge is power and power is greater than riches," he replied. "I am the first Chinese to graduate from Yale. You have the honour of being the first and only mother out of the countless millions of mothers in China at this time, who can claim the honour of having a son who is the first Chinese graduate of a first-class American college." She was very happy to hear this. Then she ordered him to shave his moustache, not appropriate for a young Chinese who was unmarried; he immediately followed her order.

He promised to look after her as best he could and saw her often for the remaining three years of her life. She died in 1858, at the age of 64. Yung was living in Shanghai at that time and returned to Xiangshan to attend her funeral.

Re-learning Chinese

In the summer of 1855, he moved to Guangzhou to re-learn the Chinese he had forgotten during his ten-year absence. He stayed in the house of an American Protestant missionary. Yung quickly picked up Cantonese, the spoken language of his childhood, but found it more difficult to master the written language; he had studied it for only four years at Morrison School.

His home was a short distance from an execution ground, where the provincial governor, Yeh Mingchen, killed those who belonged to the Red Turbans, an uprising that had controlled much of Guangdong for the previous two years. During June, July and August, Yeh's troops decapitated 75,000 people suspected of belonging to this group. Yung went to see the place.

"The ground was perfectly drenched with human blood. On both sides of the driveway were to be seen headless human trunks, piled up in heaps, waiting to be taken away for burial." The air around the site was full of the poisonous stench of the bodies. It was a horrific reminder of the country to which Wing had wanted so desperately to return.

After he returned home, "I felt faint-hearted and depressed in spirit. I had no appetite for food and, when night came, I was too nervous for sleep."

Then he worked for three months as private secretary for an American medical missionary who had been appointed the country's Commissioner – ambassador – in China. Wing earned US$15 a month but had very little to do.

Then he moved to Hong Kong, when he stayed in the house of Andrew Shortrede, a British journalist who had helped to support him during his time in the U.S.. He became an interpreter in the Hong Kong Supreme Court, at HK$75 a month and started to study law.

This caused a revolt among the British lawyers who feared that, because Yung alone mastered English and Cantonese, he would monopolize all the Chinese legal business. They succeeded in forcing him out of the field. His principal told him politely that he would have to study law somewhere – but there was no other place.

"I might have made a fortune if I had succeeded in my legal profession," he said. On the other hand, staying in Hong Kong would have prevented him from working on the larger stage of China, so he was happy to move to Shanghai in August 1856.

New life in Shanghai

He found a job as a translator in the Imperial Customs, earning 100 Mexican dollars. He left after four months in anger because he found a regular system of bribes between the translators and the Chinese shippers; the chief commissioner offered to double his salary to keep him but he felt he had to leave on this matter of principle.

Next, he became a clerk in an English tea and silk merchants. The partners dissolved the firm after six months and Yung returned to translating, at which he was gifted.

Then he was hired by the English firm, Dent and Company, as an inland agent. This would both give him a good salary and also the opportunity to travel widely in China and learn about his country. He was sent on a tour of Zhejiang, Jiangxi, Hunan and Hubei to inspect the production and sale of tea and silk. The journey, from March to October, took him seven months; it was the first time he had been through the interior of China. What he saw strengthened his conviction that the country needed radical change and that, to achieve it, he would have to enter the mainstream of society.

In the autumn of 1859, in company with two missionaries, he went to Nanjing to see the leaders of the Taiping Rebellion. "My object was to find out for my own satisfaction the character of the Taipings: whether or not they were the men fitted to set up a new government in place of the Manchu Dynasty." The party reached Nanjing.

On November 19, he had a meeting with a nephew of Hung Xiu-quan, the leader of the Taipings. Yung offered his services to the rebels if they followed seven proposals he outlined – organizing an army on scientific principles: setting up schools for military and naval officers: establishing a modern banking system and an educational system with grades, including the Bible as a textbook: setting up a system of industrial schools.

On their return to Shanghai, he wrote an assessment of the Taipings. He saw the cause of the rebellion in the deep corruption of the entire administrative system, the exploitation of the people by officials and a government "founded on a gigantic system of fraud and falsehood".

But he left bitterly disappointed as he saw the Taipings contributed no new political ideas or principles which would have constituted the foundation of a new form of government and brought no benefit to China. "The only good (that resulted from the Taiping Rebellion was) that God made use of it as a dynamic power to break the stagnancy of a great nation and wake up its consciousness for a new national life."

Yung returned to the tea trade and succeeded in bringing 65,000 boxes of tea from a Taiping-controlled area. It was a dangerous project, bringing the cargo on boats through areas rife with rebels and bandits. At the end, he fell ill for two months because of the stress.

He set up his own tea commission business and ran it for three years.

During his early years back in China, Yung found that he was caught between two worlds – he was both Chinese and western but did not belong in one world or the other. He found among the foreigners of Hong Kong and Shanghai a deep prejudice against Chinese; the Americans among whom he had lived as a student treated him better than most of the expatriates he met in China. On the other hand, many Chinese found him too westernized.

At that time, Chinese were married in their late teens or early twenties to partners chosen by their families. But he was not married because he would not have accepted such an alliance. He was an oddball, out of the mainstream.

Zeng Guo-fan

In July 1863, he received an invitation from Zeng Guo-fan（曾國藩）, Viceroy of Jiangsu, Jiangxi and Anhui provinces and the general who had played the most important role in defeating the Taiping. The rebellion lasted from 1850 to 1864 and cost about 20 million lives. Zeng was one of the most influential leaders of the government in the 19th century.

In September, Yung took a boat down the Yangtze to Nanjing to meet Zeng. It was a pivotal moment in his life. When he entered the room, Zeng looked at him with an intense, piercing gaze such as Yung had never seen. Zeng asked him for his views on China; he outlined his proposals for reform and public policy. Zeng then gave his views.

Yung was amazed; here was a man that he did not believe existed in China – someone who recognized the causes of the country's decline and the steps needed to rectify it, a man who shared his vision that China must introduce western ideas and technology and establish modern industry.

He impressed him so much that, when Zeng invited him to join the government service, he agreed and gave up his lucrative job in the private sector. He was made a mandarin of the fifth of the nine ranks in the official system. Zeng was a man he admired his whole life.

Zeng instructed him to go abroad and purchase machinery for a machine shop four miles northwest of Shanghai; it became the Jiangnan Arsenal, into which millions were invested.

He was given 68,000 taels (a Chinese unit of weight that, when applied to silver, was used as a unit of currency) for the purchase. He arrived in New York in the early spring of 1864. An American friend who was a mechanical engineer found a company to carry out the order – the Putnam Machine Co. of Fitchburg, Massachusetts.

According to Yang Yi, secretary-general of the Research Institute of Yung Wing and the Students Who Went to the U.S., Yung volunteered to fight in the U.S. army against the Confederate South. He believed that it was his duty as an American citizen. The recruiting officer turned him down, saying that he was on a mission from the Chinese government which he needed to complete. If he were killed, who would do it?

The firm needed a year to complete the order and shipped the machines directly from New York to Shanghai, via the Cape of Good Hope, in early spring 1865. They arrived in Shanghai in perfect working order; Zeng was delighted at the smooth completion of the order.

In recognition of this, Yung was in October 1865 promoted to a mandarin of the fifth rank, working as interpreter and translator, with a high salary of $250 a month. He set up a Bureau of Translation, which over the next 10 years translated over 100 works. These include Parson's *Law of Contracts*, a book of English law, large portions of Colton's Geography, books on manufacturing as well as a magazine published four times a year with reports of current events in the west.

In 1867, Zeng saw the arsenal and was delighted. Yung persuaded him to add a mechanical school to teach mechanical engineering to Chinese, to enable it to be independent of foreigners. Later, in the spring of 1873, he arranged an order of 50 Gatling guns for US$100,000; this was followed by other orders shipped to China, so that it would have the most modern weapons.

The Jiangnan Arsenal went on to become the largest weapons factory in east Asia, producing the first domestically made steam boat in 1868 and the first domestically made steel. It had the largest budgets of any arsenal set up by the reformers, at 400,000 silver taels a year. Most of the senior technical staff were westerners.

Another mission Yung completed for the government was to compile a report on the condition of Chinese labourers in Peru, which he completed in 1873 with two American friends. It took three months and involved secret photographs of the coolies taken at night; their backs were lacerated, scarred and disfigured. He sent the report to Beijing. As a result of the outrage caused by his report, the trade stopped.

In 1868, he drew up four proposals for the government. First was the organization of a joint stock steamship company, entirely Chinese-owned and operated; its steamships would carry rice from Shanghai and the south to Beijing.

The second was to send 120 students to US, in four batches of 30: aged from 12 to 14, they would have 15 years to finish their education. This scheme should be continued indefinitely.

He also proposed the start of mining and railways – but China had no mining engineers – and fourthly a ban on foreign missionaries exercising jurisdiction over their converts in either civil or criminal cases. He forwarded the four proposals to Prime Minister Wen Seang in Beijing; but he died soon after and no-one considered them.

Yung became discouraged; he lived largely on his own.

Then, during the winter of 1870, the government accepted the idea of sending the students to the U.S.. His principal argument was that, in its relations with other countries, China had few people trained to act at its representatives. As a result, many important posts, such as the management of its forts, warships, military forces and customs, were held by foreigners: to whom were they loyal?

This change of heart was due to the influence of Zeng Guo-fan and Li Hong-zhang（李鴻章）, the two most important reformers in the administration. Li was one of the most significant figures of the late Qing Dynasty; he tried to modernize China despite strong resistance in many parts of the court and the government.

The government allocated US$1.5 million to execute the project. Yung could not conceal his joy. For two days, he could neither eat nor sleep. It was 16 years since he returned to China and 20 years since he had conceived the idea. Without his determination and persistence, the scheme would never have happened.

Education project – mission of his life

In the winter of 1870, he went to Nanjing to meet Zeng and settle the details – setting up a preparatory school, number of students, where the money would come from and number of years they would stay in the U.S..

The government would pay all the fees, for study and living expenses. It established a Chinese Educational Commission; it consisted of two commissioners, Yung and Chin Lan-pin（陳蘭彬）, two Chinese teachers and one interpreter. Chin was an official of the Han Lin rank sent to see that the students kept up their knowledge of Chinese.

In exchange for paying all the fees, the government set several conditions: the students must return to China on completing their studies and work for the government. They must not cut their pigtails, convert to Christianity or have love affairs.

Initially, the government decided to send children aged 15-19 but amended this to nine-15; this was because it expected them to stay 15 years abroad before returning home. At that time, the average lifespan was 50-60 years and a man had to spend three years in mourning after the death of his father; so, if they left at 19 and returned at 34 and later spent three years in mourning, that meant a working life that would probably be less than 20 years.

Students between 12 and 15, would spend one year in a preparatory school before they went, after being selected by competitive examination. Their parents and guardians would sign a form saying they agreed to let them go for 15 years. The preparatory school was set up in Shanghai and the scheme began in the summer of 1871.

His next task was to find families willing to send their children at such a young age to this remote and unknown country. Most Chinese considered it dangerous to send their children so far away; it was like giving them up. They thought the U.S. was a country of barbarians; they had no conception of the western world.

Since China had no newspapers at that time, Yung had to recruit the students personally; he went to Guangdong and the southeast coastal areas. During a visit to his home village of Nan Ping, he donated 500 taels of silver to establish the Zhenxian school.

It was very difficult to find applicants. No family of rank or wealth would sign up, only the poor. He went to Nan Ping and neighbouring villages and spoke to relatives and friends; even then, he could not find enough. He had to go to Hong Kong and signed up several; in this way, he was able to reach the initial 30.

Most applications were Cantonese, with the largest number from Xiangshan; Yung's good name and reputation won over the parents. In total, 84 of the 120 students who went to the U.S. were from Guangdong, including 39 from Xiangshan, almost one third of the total: no wonder it was the cradle of China's modernization. Next came Jiangsu, with 22: Zhejiang with eight, Shanghai with seven, Anhui with four and Fujian with two.

Starting the mission

Yung set out with the first group of 30 on August 11, 1872. The young students felt a mixture of fear, loneliness and excitement. It was the first time they had left China; they had no idea of the strange and distant country to which they were going.

After arriving in California, they took the train to the east coast. Out of the window they saw wild animals and Indian tribesmen. They could speak almost no English and could not communicate with those around them. They arrived in Hartford, Connecticut; Yung had decided to make the headquarters of the project there.

Yung wisely decided that, as he and the other students of Morrison School had done 30 years before, the young men would adapt to American life and learn English most quickly if they stayed with local families.

A total of 132 families applied to accept the Chinese students, mostly doctors, ministers of religion, lawyers and professors. Yung decided that it would be easier for each student if he had another Chinese with him; he decided on two per family. A total of 47 families were chosen.

Their hosts treated them as members of their own family, eating with them and taking them to church on Sundays.

It was a rude awakening: everything was new. They had to get used to western food for the first time, no easy task for Chinese students even today. Like all men in the Qing Empire, they had to wear pigtails; when they went outside, they were chased by American children who called them "Chinese girls".

Not only did they have the daunting task of learning English and adapting to this strange new life, they also had to continue their Chinese studies; this was one condition for their government to approve the project.

Yung rented space in Hartford which included classrooms where they studied Chinese; this meant that their burden of homework was heavier than that of American children. In the classroom, they had to bow before images of the Emperor and of Confucius. If they did not complete their Chinese essay, the teacher beat them.

In January 1875, Yung moved into new headquarters, a spacious three-storey house large enough to accommodate the commissioners, teachers and 75 students at one time in dormitories. The Chinese government paid US$50,000 to build the headquarters; it included the classroom for the study of Chinese.

"The motive which led me to build permanent headquarters of our own was to have the educational mission as deeply rooted in the U.S. as possible, so as not to give the Chinese government any chance of retrograding in this movement," said Yung.

On the wall of the house were portraits of the three Chinese leaders who had made the project possible – Zeng Guo-fan, Li Hong-zhang and Ting Yi-tcheang, the governor of Jiangsu.

After three years, the children had enough English to go to school; their acclimatization accelerated. Like other young migrants to the U.S., they shed the skin of their former life and adopted a new one. Teased for wearing a pigtail, some cut it off; but they kept it and fastened it on when they met Qing officials. They did not wear Chinese, but American clothes.

Most lost interest in studying Chinese classics, which they saw as irrelevant, and did not want to honour Confucius or follow the rituals. They had to follow the same subjects as their American classmates – Latin, Greek, algebra, arithmetic, geography and history.

Some dated American girls and fell in love with them.

They joined their classmates in sports like basketball and football; one organized the world's first Chinese baseball team. Later, several were in the Yale rowing team which several times beat their bitter rivals from Harvard.

Some became Protestant Christians and were baptized; a few

became very devout and organized a group to convert the Chinese nation. Such conversions had been specifically forbidden by the Qing government. One of the students wrote back to his parents in China that he had converted to Christianity; it was an unwise decision. His father reported this to the government, which ordered him to return home at once, because he had broken one of the three prohibitions. Chinese officials took him to the railway station for the journey home but he did not take the train and remained in the U.S. for the rest of his life.

By the late 1870s, they had started to graduate from secondary school and enter university; many went to Yale, as Yung had done.

As he watched their progress, Yung was overjoyed: "when the young men arrived in New England, the heavy weight of repression and suppression was lifted from their minds; they exulted in their freedom and leapt for joy. No wonder they took to athletic sports with alacrity and delight."

He was realizing his life's work. His plan was to create an educated elite that would reform and modernize China. He wanted it to be a permanent project, allowing thousands of students to come and receive a western education which they would put to the service of their country.

Mission aborted

Things went smoothly for the first four years. Yung had a good relationship with the other commissioner, Chin Lan-pin, the man sent by the Qing government to look after its interests.

In 1876, Chin returned to China and was replaced by Wu Zi-deng (吳子登). While he supported the project in principle, he was more traditional, representing the conservative faction in the court. On his arrival, he was shocked by what he found, especially the Americanization of the students; he felt that they were losing their "Chineseness".

When he discovered that two had become Christian – in defiance of the official orders – he ordered them to go home. Knowing the punishment that awaited them, the two ignored the order and, with the help of friends, continued their studies.

Wu severely criticized those who had cut off their pigtails and ordered an increase in the education given in Chinese and the study of traditional rites. It was a mirror of the fierce debate raging in China itself, of tradition against reform, of classical education against western learning.

After five years in the U.S., the students had formed their own opinions. They did not want to follow Wu and only listened to Yung. The two men become bitter enemies. Wu decided that the students should not be allowed to remain in the U.S. because they would be "lost" to China and started to campaign for this in the Imperial Court; he wrote letters to Li Hong-zhang, the official in charge of foreign affairs.

While Yung understood things American, Wu was his superior in Chinese politics; he knew how to lobby and campaign in the corridors of power in Beijing. Yung was completely out of his depth.

In his letters, Wu argued that the mission had failed because it had turned the young men into Americans who would not serve their country but their foreign masters: the only way to rescue the situation was to recall all the students, even though most were in the middle of school and university courses. Much of the information he gave was misleading and untrue.

Yung also had his supporters in Beijing; but he did not understand the workings of Chinese politics nor how to respond. He did not know how to compose the right kind of letter or the right channels through which to send it. He defended himself against the accusations but with limited success. Of his three backers, Zeng Guo-fan had died in March 1872 and Li was not as strong as he had been 10 years before; he was wavering.

What tipped the scales in Wu's favour was the refusal of the U.S. State Department to allow Chinese to study at West Point and the Naval Academy at Annapolis, the most important colleges for the American army and navy. Japanese students were admitted.

China desperately needed to modernize its military if it ever were to withstand the foreign powers encroaching on its resources and sovereignty. For Wu and the conservatives in the court, this refusal was the proof of American prejudice and hostility against China.

It came at a time of rising anti-Chinese sentiment in the U.S., mainly among white working class people who saw Chinese as a threat to their jobs, status and wages.

This fear of the "Yellow Peril" led to the *Page Act of 1875* and the *Chinese Exclusion Act of 1882*, which banned "skilled and unskilled Chinese labourers and those working in mining" for 10 years.

In 1881, the government ordered the return of all the students; only three had graduated from university.

Yung did not take accept this decision; he mobilized his many contacts in the U.S. to campaign on his behalf.

Senior figures wrote a letter of protest to the Chinese Office for Foreign Affairs, including Rev Noah Porter, President of Yale.

The letter praised the good behaviour and hard work of the students. "As a result of their good conduct, many of the prejudices of ignorant and wicked men toward the Chinese have been removed and more favourable sentiments have taken their place." It asked that the decision be reconsidered.

After being approached by an intermediary on Yung's behalf, former President Ulysses Grant wrote a letter to Li Hong-zhang; Li wanted the students to stay but the conservative faction in the court was too powerful.

The appeals failed. The return to Shanghai took place in June and August 1881. Fewer than 20 disobeyed the order and remained in the U.S.. The 96 who returned were locked in a study hall in Shanghai to re-learn their "Chineseness". They were not allowed out, even for the mid-autumn festival. After a stay there, they were assigned jobs. One was sent to teach English in Guangzhou.

The study of many was abruptly terminated in the middle, leaving them unable to graduate; but, despite this, the returnees made great contributions to their country in different fields – mining, railways, telecommunications, education, diplomacy, commerce and the military.

Although the programme lasted only nine years, it had a profound impact on China, not only through the achievements of the returnees but the example it set to tens of thousands of Chinese in the future, who would go to the U.S. and other countries to learn new skills and ways of thinking. Yung could be proud of what he had achieved.

With the passage of the *Chinese Exclusion Act of 1882*, support in Beijing for such a study programme ended.

Of the 120 students, one died, seven returned for different reasons and the remaining 112 completed their course or were studying when the project ended.

Broken-hearted

Yung was heart-broken by the cancellation of the project. It was the mission of his life to bring Chinese students to the U.S.; he had devoted 20 years to bring it to fruition and now saw it torpedoed by the conservatism and xenophobia of the Qing court.

Nonetheless, as a loyal official of the government, he returned with the students to China and visited his superiors. He spent three months in Beijing and drew up a plan for the suppression of the Indian opium trade in China and abolition of poppy cultivation in China and India. He submitted it to the government but it was never implemented. As in many things, Yung was years ahead of his compatriots.

In late 1882, he rushed back to his home in Hartford, Connecticut to take care of his American wife.

He had first been married in 1868, to a lady named Zheng from Suzhou to whom he had been introduced by a friend. Yung was 40, an advanced age for a Chinese man of that era to marry – one result of his very atypical life. Most Chinese had marriages arranged by their families in their late teens.

But this marriage did not last after Yung went to the U.S. with the students. Madame Zheng remained in China and never went abroad; she died in 1911.

In March 1875, he married Mary Kellogg, an American woman of 24, to whom he was introduced by a friend. He was 47. She was the love of his life.

They had two sons – Morrison Brown born in 1876 and Bartlett, born in 1879. It was to look after his wife that he returned to Hartford in the spring of 1883; he had been away for nearly 18 months. "I found my wife in a very low condition. She had lost the use of her voice and greeted me in a low hoarse whisper. She was much emaciated."

This was due in part to her anxiety over his safety in China and fears of retaliation against him over the student mission.

Over the next three years, he did his best to improve her health by taking her to warmer and cleaner cities in the U.S.. But he could not save her. She died of acute nephritis, a kidney disease, on June 28, 1886 and was buried in the Cedar Hill cemetery, in Hartford. She was only 35 and they had been married for 11 years.

It was a second devastating blow, after the failure of the student mission. "Her death made a great void in my life, which was irreparable, but she did not leave me hopelessly deserted and alone; she left me two sons who are constant reminders of her beautiful life and character."

For the next 10 years, he devoted most of his time to their upbringing and education, aided by Mary Bartlett, his mother-in-law, who kept his house for nearly two years.

Both his sons followed their father's footsteps and went to study at Yale.

War with Japan

While he lived in the U.S., he continued to follow closely events in his homeland. Things went from bad to worse. After 25 years of rapid industrial and military modernization, Japan wanted to follow the example of the European colonial powers.

They had exploited the weakness and chaos of China, so Japan would also. Hostilities broke out in July 1894, over which country would control Korea. The Japanese forces won one victory after another.

"My sympathies were enlisted on the side of China, not because I am a Chinese but because China had the right on her side and Japan was simply trumping up a pretext to go to war," he wrote.

So he came up with a plan – negotiate a loan of US$15 million from banks in London to buy three or four iron-clad battleships that were ready for action and a foreign force of 5,000 men. This force would attack Japan on the Pacific coast, to create a diversion to draw the Japanese troops from Korea and give China time to recruit a new army and navy.

In addition, the government would set up a commission to mortgage Formosa (Taiwan) to a western power for US$400 million to be spent on a national army and navy to carry out the war.

To Yung's great surprise, the government approved the first part of the plan in the winter of 1894. It was a sign of its desperation and inability to defeat Japan's forces; it would have to depend on a foreign soldiers and sailors to do it.

So Yung went to London and negotiated the loan; the banks made the condition that China provide its customs revenue as collateral. They were deeply suspicious of the efficiency and probity of the Qing government but had confidence in the customs department that was under a British inspector-general, Robert Hart.

There the deal stalled. The court in Beijing was divided over whether to accept the deal. Hart was obliged to follow the peace faction supported by the Empress Dowager; to gain peace would involve paying a substantial sum in reparations, so Hart refused to use the customs revenue that would be needed to pay the reparations. So the loan was never made.

Yung heard no more of his plan to mortgage Formosa.

The war ended in total victory for Japan which took over Korea and captured the southern part of Liaoning province and the port of Weihaiwei in Shandong province. Under the *Treaty of Shimonoseki*（馬關條約） signed on April 17, 1895, China recognized the total independence of Korea and ceded southern Liaoning, Taiwan and the Penghu Islands to Japan. It also paid 200 million Kuping taels in war reparations; that was equivalent to six times the annual revenue of the Japanese government.

Silent Viceroy

The defeat by Japan stunned China and the world which had expected a comfortable Chinese victory. Historically, Japan was a tributary state – how could this disaster have occurred? How could a small island country with few resources defeat the great Qing Empire?

Like many others, Yung believed that this would open the way for radical reforms of the sort which he had been advocating for 30 years.

So, after entrusting his two sons to the care of his brother-in-law, he decided to return to China in the expectation that the defeat had changed the mindset of the senior officials of the Qing government and made them ready to accept new ideas.

In the early summer of 1895, he arrived in Shanghai; he had to spend heavily on a complete set of official robes. He went to Nanjing to meet the Viceroy of Jiangsu and Zhejiang, Chang Chi-tung, and laid out one of his typically ambitious proposals.

The government should appoint four foreigners as advisers to the departments of Foreign Affairs, Treasury, Army and Navy; they would be men of practical experience, ability and character and given contracts for 10 years that could be renewed. Their advice should be taken up and acted upon.

Young and able Chinese students would be chosen to work under them. In this way, the government would gradually be rebuilt on western lines. Anything that Japan could do China could do better.

The Viceroy listened impassively to Yung's passionate presentation. He expressed no opinion on any of the proposals. The encounter could not have been more different to that with Zeng Guo-fan in 1863, which had so inspired the young returnee. He never met Chang again.

He was given the post of Secretary of Foreign Affairs from Jiangnan, with a monthly salary of US$150. But he was not invited to meetings or to give his opinion on policy; it was obvious that his services were not required.

So, after three months in Nanjing, he resigned his post and moved to Shanghai; no longer an official, he was free to speak and write as he wished.

National bank

His next proposal was the establishment of a National Bank, with an initial sum of 10 million taels.

He prepared the text with great care, using U.S. banking legislation and then presenting it to two senior officials of the Treasury Department, including the President, Ung Tung Hwo. They helped him greatly, removing clauses that were inapplicable to China.

It was these two officials that presented the proposal to the government. The project went forward: a committee was set up to select a site for the bank and Yung asked to go to the U.S. to consult with the Treasury Department in Washington on the proposal.

But the idea was torpedoed by the intervention of Sheng Xuan-huai (盛宣懷), one of China's richest and most powerful entrepreneurs. His spies in Beijing had kept him informed of the project, which he judged against his interests.

According to Yung, Sheng came to Beijing and paid 300,000 taels in bribes to two to three princes and other high officials. They cancelled the project and allocated the 10 million taels to Sheng to set up his own bank.

"The defeat of the National Banking project owed its origin to the thoroughly corrupt condition of the administrative system of China. From the Dowager Empress down to the lowest and most petty underling in the Empire, the whole political fabric was honey-combed with graft … with money, one could get anything done in China."

Two railways

Undeterred by his setback, Yung then proposed another project – building a railway line of 500 miles between the port of Tianjin on the Bohai Gulf and Zhenjiang on the Yangtze River in Jiangsu province.

The government awarded him the concession, on condition that it be built with Chinese capital and that he secure this within six months. No Chinese entrepreneur would fund such a scheme, so he had to raise money from foreign companies. Unfortunately, he was unable to obtain the funding and had to give up the idea.

Coup d'état

During his time in Beijing, Yung met Kang You-wei（康有為）, Liang Chi-chao（梁啟超） and other reformers who were close to the young Emperor Guangxu. His reign began in 1875, when he was four; in practice, he ruled, under the influence of the Empress Dowager Cixi Taihou（慈禧太后）, from 1889 to 1908.

Yung shared many of the ideals and views of the reformers.

In June 1898, the emperor launched a series of sweeping political, legal and social changes, the most far-reaching of the Qing. These included the building of a modern university in Beijing, the construction of railways and a system of budgeting similar to that of the west. His aim was to follow the example of Japan and make China a constitutional monarchy.

He also dismissed hundreds of court and government officials he considered superfluous.

The conservative forces within the government, led by the Empress Dowager, were outraged; for them, the reforms were drastic and dangerous. She organized a military coup. In September, troops surrounded the Imperial Palace and arrested the emperor. She issued an edict, saying that Guangxu was not fit to be emperor; his reign had effectively ended.

The coup organizers started a witch hunt against the reformers. Some were executed in public and others fled, Yung among them. The government offered a large reward for his capture.

"Being implicated by harbouring the reformers and in deep sympathy with them, I had to flee for my life and succeeded in escaping from Beijing. I took up quarters in the foreign settlement of Shanghai," he wrote. There he organized a national association to discuss the leading questions of the day, especially reform; he was chosen as the first president.

In 1899, he was advised, for his personal safety, to move. So he moved to the safety of the British colony of Hong Kong.

In the spring of 1901, he visited Taiwan and met its governor, Gentaro Kodama（兒玉源太郎）, one of the founders of the Imperial Japanese Army. With a smile, Kodama told him that the Chinese government had asked him to arrest Yung and hand him over. "I am not going to play the part of a constable for China, so you may rest at ease on this point."

Kodama then brought out a Chinese newspaper with a report of the plan to mortgage Taiwan to raise money to fight Japan and asked Yung if he was the author. He said that he was and described the details. "Should like circumstances ever arise, nothing would deter me from repeating the same proposition in order to fight Japan." he said.

Kodama was delighted at this frankness and assigned him four bodyguards to give him 24-hour protection during his short visit, to prevent an assassination attempt. He also invited him to visit Japan and to meet the Emperor and other leading personalities.

"This interview was one of the most memorable of my life," he recalled. Instead of being handed over to the Qing government or arrested by the Japanese, he was treated like a VIP.

Final years

In 1898, U.S. Secretary of State John Sherman informed him that the U.S. citizenship he had held for 50 years had been revoked and that he would not be allowed to return. He made this decision despite the fact that

Yung submitted a certified copy of his naturalization certificate and several passports issued by the State Department.

"A refusal to admit now his right to privileges which he has apparently exercised for many years would on its face seem unjust and without warrant," wrote Sherman in his decision. "Nevertheless, in view of the construction placed upon the naturalization laws of the U.S. by our highest courts, the Department does not feel that it can properly recognize him as a citizen of the United States."

Sherman was referring to the *Chinese Exclusion Act of 1882*.

However, with the help of friends, Yung returned from Hong Kong illegally; he arrived in time to see his second son, Bartlett, graduate from Yale in 1902.

Thereafter Yung lived in poverty at his home in Hartford.

In May 1911, Yung suffered a stroke at home.

He was excited by the success of the revolution in 1911 and Dr. Sun invited him to return but he was too old. He asked his two sons to go to China and serve the country.

Yung died on April 21, 1912 at his home in Hartford, aged 84 and was buried next to his wife in the Cedar Hill cemetery on the city outskirts. At the funeral, the minister read a homily: "If he had not been old, he would certainly have taken part in the revolution. He was fiercely loyal to China until the end of his life."

Tributes and Legacy

In April, 1933 Jiaotong University in Shanghai opened the Yung Wing Memorial building with 62 rooms at a cost of 131.8 million Chinese yuan. It was the main administrative building of the university and had a copper statue of Yung on its second floor. The statue was later moved to the history museum of the university.

In 1998, John Rowland, governor of Connecticut, named September 22 as Memorial Day for Yung Wing and the Chinese students.

Yung's statue was put in the Hall of Fame at Yale on May 5, with George Bush and Bill Clinton.

A public elementary school in New York's Chinatown is named after him.

Zhuhai has a nursery and two schools named after him. And Zhongshan University in Guangzhou has a statue of him. .

His home village of Nan Ping is now part of the special economic zone of Zhuhai. In the midst of broad highways and expensive skyscraper apartment blocks, part of the original village remains, including the Zhenxian (甄賢, Examining Virtue) primary school which he established with 500 taels of his money in 1871.

He went there for the last time in 1902, when he was on the run from the government and just before his escape abroad. He asked that the school change to a western-style curriculum. This was done in 1906 and Yung was made honorary principal – even though he was in exile.

The school was expanded with other buildings and a large exercise space added until 2007, when it closed and moved to a new site.

The original building has become the Yung Wing museum, with a statue of the founder in front. "The plan was for the rest of the school to become a museum to the students who went to the U.S.," said the school guardian. "But the money for this has not arrived, so the buildings remain closed." Zhuhai is one of the richest cities in China, in per capita terms, and the site of thousands of empty apartments; so this lack of finance is hard to understand and suggests a lack of respect for the city's most famous son.

Indeed, the museum is extremely hard to find – there are no signposts and few people, even in the village, know of its existence; and it is inside premises that are locked and has no external signboard.

That said, the museum itself is evocative – six classrooms in a one-storey grey brick building that Yung established because he wanted the children of his home village to have an education even if their families were not wealthy.

It is full of photographs and material about Yung and the students he took with him to the U.S.. They are smartly dressed in the suits and neckties of wealthy young Americans but their facial expressions are of unease and uncertainty, as if they are asking if the clothes fit the person wearing them. "Do I belong here? Am I a Chinese or an American?"

There are photographs of the sturdy college buildings and apartment blocks where they lived and studied and of the American families and teachers, many of them devout Christians, who took them in. They were the kind and sympathetic face of western colonialism; many remained in contact with their Chinese guests for the whole of their lives.

One photograph shows the imposing four-storey structure in Hartford that was the headquarters of Yung's educational mission; it was built to last for a hundred years – not the 11 he was given by the Qing government.

Also on display is a list of the students who went, their names, birthdays and native places. More than half came from Guangdong province and a large proportion from Xiangshan. The slogan on the boards is "教育救國", "education saves the country": it was the lifetime credo of Yung for himself, the young people of China and the country itself.

Other photos feature Yung with fellow alumni of Yale in 1894 and the modest home at 16 Atwood, Hartford, where he lived for his final years, and of his grave and tombstone in the town.

There are also images of some of the 1,800 Chinese who studied in the U.S. with scholarships from the Boxer Indemnity (funded by money paid in reparations to the U.S. after the suppression of the Boxer Rebellion); others went to Britain, France, Germany, Belgium and Russia. They were all, in one sense, "children" of Yung.

Yung Wing on his graduation from Yale University.

Mary Kellogg, the American wife of Yung Wing.

The first group of students sent by the Qing government to the United
States, photographed in Shanghai in 1872 before their departure.

The Zhenxian (Examining Virtue) primary school which Yung Wing established in Xiangshan in 1871, with a statue of him at the front door.

The Yung Wing College in present-day Zhuhai.

Chapter Two

黄寬
1829 - 1878

Pioneer Doctor
Huang Kuan

Introduction

When Yung Wing set off for the United States on that vessel in January 1847, he had two classmates with him from the Morrison School. One was Huang Sheng, who returned to China the next year because of poor health. The other was Huang Kuan, the subject of this chapter.

We know less about him than the other sons of Xiangshan who studied overseas. This is because he died at the young age of 49 and left few records of himself; instead, he wrote widely on medical subjects for professional journals. He translated a large amount of medical material from Chinese into English. He had a very busy life as a surgeon, general practitioner and teacher of medicine. This left him little time to write a diary or memoirs. In addition, he had no children or heirs – leaving no-one to collect his belongings and celebrate his achievements.

What we know is dramatic enough. That August morning in 1846, he was one of the only three students brave enough to take up the challenge of Reverend Samuel Brown to go to the U.S.. He seized the opportunity with both hands. After completing secondary school at Monson Academy in Massachusetts, he went on to study medicine at the University of Edinburgh in Scotland, one of the world's leading institutions in this field. He was the first Chinese to be trained as a western doctor and the first Chinese to graduate from a university in Europe.

Then he returned home and had a distinguished career. At that time, China had only a few hundred western-trained doctors, the vast majority of them foreigners. He was an outstanding doctor in Guangzhou, performing thousands of operations, including the first caesarean section in China. For 19 years, he worked at the city's Boji Hospital, one of the most famous medical institutions in the country, of which he was director when its American chief was absent. Chinese and foreigners who wanted an operation sought him out. He was also a pioneer in medical education, helping to set up the country's first medical school. When the China Customs department picked 17 doctors for its new medical service, it chose only one Chinese – Huang Kuan. His life was short, but he left a deep footprint.

Childhood

Huang was born in Dongan village (東岸鄉), one of several villages comprising Tangjiawan township, in 1829; we do not know the exact date. His parents died when he was very young and he was raised by his grandmother. An intelligent boy, he went to a local private school and attracted the attention of the teachers by his excellent memory; but, because of the poverty of his family, he had to drop out.

In 1841, at the age of 12, he went to Macao to study at the school established there in memory of the first Protestant missionary to China, Robert Morrison. He was one of the first six students. When the school re-located to Hong Kong in 1842, Huang moved with it; he spent six years at the school and learnt English; he achieved excellent results. In Hong Kong, the school expanded and had more than 40 students.

One day in August 1846, the principal, Reverend Brown, got up in class and said that, because of the poor health of himself and his wife, he had decided to return to the U.S. and wished to take three to five students with him. Yung was the first to stand up to offer himself as a candidate, followed by Huang Sheng and Huang Kuan. Brown asked that the three obtain the permission of their parents to go. In this regard, perhaps Huang Kuan had more freedom than the other two, since his parents had died and he needed the approval of only his grandmother.

The fees for the three students were paid for two years by three foreigners living in Hong Kong – an American businessman named

Ritchie, a Scotsman named Campbell and Andrew Shortrede, a Scottish publisher who had founded the *China Mail* newspaper in February 1845. After a successful publishing career in Edinburgh, Shortrede moved to Hong Kong in 1843-44. A man of learning, he drafted in 1847 the by-laws of the Royal Asiatic Society in Hong Kong and was one of the founders of the Saint Andrew's School in the colony in 1855; it was the first school there not run by missionaries and to be funded by public subscription.

On January 4, 1847, Huang set off from Hong Kong with Rev Brown and his wife and two other Chinese students to New York, where they arrived on April 12; he was 18. They entered Monson Academy in Massachusetts, from which they graduated in 1850. This was one of the United States' elite secondary schools, which prepared students for university; its principal, Reverend Charles Hammond, a graduate of Yale, paid special attention to his three new Chinese students. They lived in the house of the mother of Reverend Brown and had to do part-time jobs to help cover their costs.

Huang Sheng returned to China because of ill-health in 1848. Huang Kuan and Yung graduated after two years, in 1849.

When he had first arrived, Huang had no expectation of what he would do after graduation, other than return to China and try to find a job.

Going to Edinburgh

At this point, Shortrede and Huang's other benefactors in Hong Kong said that, if he wished to go to study at the University of Edinburgh, Shortrede's hometown, they would be willing to support him. The money would come from British businessmen in the colony and members of the Edinburgh Medical Missionary Society.

Academically, this was a wonderful opportunity for the young man. Edinburgh was one of the most famous universities in Europe and he was being offered tuition and board at no cost. Personally, however, it was an enormous challenge. He had just learnt to adapt to one foreign country and would have to go to another, with its own particular culture and traditions; and he would have to go on his own, without the support of the two compatriots who had accompanied him to the U.S..

He was going to a city where he knew no-one and there were almost no Chinese. The climate was bleak, with a long, cold winter; it was much different from that of his native Guangdong, as was its cuisine.

Despite these obstacles, the young man took the plunge; such a golden opportunity would not come again. He crossed the Atlantic and entered the university in 1850.

Founded in 1583, it was in the 18th century a leading centre of the European Enlightenment and one of the foremost universities in Europe. The faculty of medicine was established in 1726 and the Royal Infirmary, a public hospital, opened in 1729 before moving to a new facility in 1741.

By 1764, the number of medical students had increased to the point that a new 200-seat anatomy theatre was built. It attracted students from Ireland, the Americas and British colonies; many of its graduates were closely involved in establishing the first medical schools in the U.S., Canada and – as we shall see – in China.

It was the first western institution to recruit students from China. Now about 800 students from China, Taiwan, Macao and Hong Kong attend the university every year; its recent Chinese alumni include Professor Zhong Nanshan, a native of Nanjing and one of the mainland's leading medical scientists. He became a national figure in 2003 when he and his team developed the treatment for the SARS virus.

For his first year, Huang studied literature, before switching to medicine in 1851. It was a gruelling course, especially for someone working in his second language. His classes included anatomy, chemistry, surgery, midwifery, botany, pathology, pharmacy and practical physics. He had a heavy load of academic and practical work.

He graduated in 1855, finishing third in the exam and earning a gold medal for his academic work. He was the first Chinese to graduate from a university in Europe. On graduation, he remained at the university hospital for an internship and doctorate programmes. In 1857, he obtained a Ph.D in pathology and anatomy, the first Chinese to earn a doctorate in the U.K..

He had joined a privileged elite; the number of medical doctors in Britain was small. If he had chosen to stay there, he could have enjoyed a comfortable life. But he decided to go back to China, after living in Edinburgh for seven years and abroad for 10 years.

The journey home took 166 days. "On January 3, 300 miles from the Taiwan Straits, we encountered a very fierce wind, which shook the ship up and down," he wrote in a journal. "I thank the merciful God that, after 12 days of danger, we landed safely at my home place."

He left Britain a strong Christian. For 16 years, he had studied in institutions with an intense religious atmosphere. The generosity of the foreign donors was driven both by a charitable desire to give him the benefits of a western education and by missionary zeal; they wanted him to spread the gospel in China.

Hong Kong

He arrived in Hong Kong and found his first job at a hospital founded by a missionary society.

He was disappointed by what he found. He had a Ph.D from one of the most prestigious medical schools in the west and was a Christian; this should have made him the equal of the foreign doctors there. But it did not.

They were accustomed to working with Chinese as assistants who had limited medical training and who followed the instructions of their superiors. Just 20 years after its establishment, Hong Kong was a very unequal society; prejudice against Chinese among the British was widespread.

So Huang resigned and took a management post at a private hospital.

He stayed in Hong Kong for only one year before he decided to move to Guangzhou, where he would live for the rest of his life. His experience in the colony greatly weakened his religious belief; he had expected better treatment from the missionary doctors who did not practise the charity and equality they preached. He was also disappointed by the infighting between different Protestant denominations.

As a result, he would devote the rest of his life to curing the sick and to medical education but not evangelization.

Guangzhou

After his arrival in Guangzhou in 1858, Huang opened a pharmacy and clinic in Fuxue Dong Street.

He was invited to work in Hui Ai, a hospital established in the western suburb of Jinlipu by Benjamin Hobson, a British medical missionary who had been sent to China in 1839 by the London Missionary Society. In 1859, the hospital had 80 beds and received 26,030 out-patients. Hobson was active in translating medical material into China and took on a small number of students for training as doctors.

Huang agreed to work there. But his stay was short, because he had differences of opinion with its management and was unhappy with the behaviour of some missionaries. So he left in 1860 to return to private practice.

That year, he moved to another missionary hospital, Boji, where he would work for the rest of his life. His name is intimately associated with it.

Boji Hospital

This was set up in 1835 by Peter Parker, an American missionary doctor, as an eye hospital. It was the first western medical hospital in China and became one of the most important missionary hospitals in the whole country.

Its English name was Canton Hospital, but Boji is more elegant – it means "giving aid to all".

Born in Framingham, Massachusetts in 1804, Parker received degrees in medicine and theology from Yale University. In February 1834, he travelled to Guangzhou as the first full-time Protestant medical missionary to China.

At the new hospital, he specialized in diseases of the eye, including cataracts, and also removed tumours. He also introduced anesthesia in the form of sulphuric ether. Although it was intended mainly to treat eye diseases, the staff could not exclude patients suffering from other illnesses; over 2,000 were admitted during the first year.

Parker trained Chinese students in medicine and surgery; he often preached to the patients.

The hospital closed in June 1840 because of the Opium War

and re-opened in November 1842. It was as crowded as before. In 1855, because Parker became a diplomat, another American missionary doctor, John Glasgow Kerr, took over.

In 1856, because of the Second Opium War between Britain and China, it was destroyed by fire. In November 1858, Kerr returned from a visit to the U.S. and found a good building in Zengsha Street close to the river in the southern district of Guangzhou – now Huilong Street close to Haizhu Square. It opened on January 1, 1859, with seven wards and beds for 60 patients, divided between men and women.

Huang joined the hospital in 1860 and became the most important assistant to Dr. Kerr. He filled this role for the rest of his life, helping him with complicated operations and diseases and handling major administrative challenges.

With its surgical knives, needles and powerful drugs that could put you to sleep, western medicine was something bizarre and incomprehensible to the majority of Chinese. It was the opposite of Chinese medicine, which relies on herbs and plants and external treatments that are visible.

People hostile to the "red-head big-noses" accused the foreigners of removing the organs and other body parts from Chinese, including children, for their own evil purposes; such rumours could lead to street protests and sometimes violence against hospitals and missionaries.

Since the majority of western doctors were foreigners, such rumours were not hard to spread. Many did not want to entrust the health of their loved ones to these people, especially if they could not speak directly to them and only through an interpreter.

As a Chinese and a Cantonese, Huang was accessible to the people of Guangzhou. He was one of them and could speak their language. As his reputation as a doctor and surgeon grew, many people sought him out, including Chinese who lived abroad and came home for treatment.

In 1860, at the Boji Hospital, he performed the first caesarean section in China. Normally, Chinese women did not like male doctors to be present when they gave birth; but, in this case, the mother allowed it because of the complications of her pregnancy.

Huang also specialized in the removal of bladder stones; many people in Guangzhou suffered from this condition. During his career, he performed more than 3,000 operations to remove them.

He and Kerr were pioneers in surgery in China.

New site

In 1863, Kerr decided that the hospital should move to a new, larger site. He put Huang and two other colleagues in charge of supervising the construction. They moved into the new premises on October 1, 1866.

In April 1867, Kerr had to return to the U.S. for health reasons and appointed Huang as director. For the first time, all the staff were Chinese. Huang was director from April to December, the first Chinese to run a western hospital in China.

In 1867, the hospital added a pharmacist's room, a temporary patient area and a church which also served as a reception hall; it could seat 200-300 people. In 1869, a building for doctors' apartments was completed.

The hospital was treating more than 26,000 patients a year. In

1873, it added two new areas for patients, taking the number to 14. Wealthier people could have a separate room for one tael of silver per month. In 1877, the hospital designated one area for opium patients, with space for over 250.

Huang was fortunate to work with someone as capable and dedicated as Dr. Kerr, who worked at the hospital for 47 years and treated almost one million patients. Dr. Kerr performed 480,000 surgical operations, including 1,300 to remove kidney stones.

Among the many Chinese students Dr. Kerr taught was Sun Yat-sen, a student in 1886. Kerr translated 34 volumes of medical material into Chinese. He also pioneered mental health care in China, opening in 1898 the Canton Refuge for the Insane, the first mental hospital in China where he served until his death in 1901. He is buried in the Protestant cemetery outside Guangzhou, near three missionary colleagues.

Teaching

Both Huang and Kerr wanted to pass their knowledge to Chinese students.

In 1863, they accepted four students. Immediately after moving to the new site in 1866, the two established a medical teaching division, which marked the formal start of this work. They aimed to train students at the Boji and Hui Ai hospitals and a small number of outside students; they hoped that their graduates would go to work all over the Chinese empire.

In 1866, they set up the Nanhua（南華）Medical School, which was the first in China to train Chinese doctors in western medicine. Huang conducted the anatomy, physiology and surgery classes, while Kerr taught pharmaceutics and chemistry. It involved an enormous amount of translation, not only to render English medical terms into Chinese but also to find the appropriate characters for them; none had existed before. It was difficult and complicated: Huang devoted a great deal of his time to this.

Huang wrote a three-year elementary theoretical curriculum and a two-year clinical internship. Initially, Nanhua accepted only male students but in 1879, it accepted three female students, the first such school to do so in China – years ahead of medical schools in Europe.

Huang expanded the laboratories and set up a room for specimens. He was very popular with his students and worked closely with them.

One major problem was the shortage of bodies for autopsies. Chinese opposed the use of corpses of their loved ones for dissection; but they were more flexible with the bodies of children.

Huang and Kerr turned out the first generation of western doctors in China. They established a new system to train doctors and nurses that was used all over the country. It was a milestone in China.

It evolved into Lingnan University Medical School and lives on today as Sun Yat-sen University Medical and Science School, named after its most famous alumnus.

All this gave Huang a heavy clinical and teaching burden. He was less interested in evangelization, which remained for the missionary doctors a key part of their work.

Official posts

Huang's fame reached the imperial court in Beijing. He was invited by Li Hong-zhang, one of its most senior officials, to work as a doctor in the government.

In early 1862, he accepted the invitation and took up a post in Tianjin. But he resigned after less than six months because he could not accept the lifestyle and customs of an official. Ding Yu-sheng, the Governor of Shanghai, urged him to reconsider, offering him many kinds of benefits, but he refused. He returned to clinical work and teaching in Guangzhou.

In 1863, the Chinese Customs set up a medical service in Hong Kong. It recruited 17 western doctors, of whom Huang was the only Chinese. It was a sign of the high regard in which he was held by the medical profession.

Their task was to examine incoming and outgoing goods for disease and infection and to treat sick sailors. Guangzhou was one of the busiest foreign trade ports in China, with a large volume of goods and people coming in and out; Huang's duties were onerous.

When a cholera epidemic broke out in Guangzhou in 1873, he made important contributions to diagnosing and containing the disease.

In 1875, he became joint chairman of the Southwest Medical Bureau.

Passing

In October 1878, he fell ill of an infected boil. The wife of the British ambassador was having difficulties with her pregnancy and asked him to help. After declining three times, Huang finally attended her. She came through but his condition worsened and he died on October 12, 1878, at the age of 49.

Huang lived a simple life, dedicated to his patients and his teaching. Not one for socializing, he neither drank nor smoked.

He lived with his elder sister and took good care of his grandmother. For a brief time he was married to a lady named He Fu-tang but they separated, for reasons we do not know, and he never re-married.

He wrote medical papers, such as about the 1873 cholera epidemic in Guangzhou and in the annual reports of the Customs Medical Service, but little about his own life.

His passing was a major loss to Dr. Kerr and the Boji Hospital. In his praise of him, Kerr said: "He was an example of the mixture of culture between China and Britain and a model of friendship between the peoples of the two countries."

In his tribute, Wing Yung said: "He graduated third in his class in the University of Edinburgh and was an outstanding person in the medical world. His wisdom and technical ability made many people admire him. He was an outstanding surgeon. When he died, Chinese and foreigners alike mourned him. He was very popular with foreigners."

Present day

Huang Kuan is remembered today in his hometown of Zhuhai (of which Dongan village is now a part) and in Edinburgh, the city where he studied.

In March 2007, Professor Sir Timothy O'Shea, principal of the University of Edinburgh, went to Zhuhai and presented the city government with transcripts of Huang's examination results and a 68-page graduation research paper which Huang wrote in English. O'Shea also gave the city a photocopy of Huang's graduation report. "We are very proud of our connections with your region," O'Shea said.

In September that same year back in the Scottish capital Professor O'Shea unveiled a bronze statue of Huang, donated by the Zhuhai government, outside the Confucius Institute for Scotland on the university campus.

Among those present was Alex Salmond, the First Minister of Scotland.

"Huang Kuan was the very first Chinese to study in any European country," Salmond said. "We have experienced the historical association with countries like Scotland and China, both countries with deep historical knowledge. It means a great deal."

Wang Yong-da, minister/counsellor of the education section of the Chinese embassy in London, said: "He represented the older generation like us, who studied abroad to save and serve the country. From this point of view, it is absolutely meaningful to raise the statue here."

The University of Edinburgh where Huang Kuan studied.

Boji Hospital in Guangzhou where Huang Kuan worked.

A statue of Huang Kuan that stands outside the Confucius Institute at the University of Edinburgh.

Chapter Three

唐廷樞
1832 - 1892

Mr. Enterprise
Tang Ting-shu

Introduction

Tang was one of the outstanding Chinese entrepreneurs of the 19th century. He worked for the British company Jardine, Matheson before moving to government service for the last 20 years of his life.

He established many firsts – China's first shipping line, coal mine, railway line, insurance company, oil well and cable line. He did all this in the face of fierce competition from foreign companies that dominated many sectors of China's economy and opposition from many in the imperial government in Beijing, including the Empress Dowager; they regarded modernization as a mortal threat to Chinese culture and traditions.

He left a permanent legacy. More than 120 years after his death, two of the companies in which he played a major role have survived China's wars and revolutions and become major conglomerates in coal, shipping and transport, holding an important place in the national economy.

The China Merchants Group (CMG), founded in 1872 and of which he was the first general manager, has developed and grown into one of China's most important port, shipping and logistics companies, with assets totalling 392 billion yuan at the end of 2012. It is the oldest mainland Chinese firm operating in Hong Kong.

The Kailuan Group, which he established as the Kaiping Coal Mine in 1878, has grown into the sixth largest coal conglomerate in China. The reserves which Tang developed below the ground in Hebei province are still being mined today.

He was one of several entrepreneurs in his family. His brother and two cousins also went into business, as did his nephew and grand-nephew. Four members of the family, including Tang himself, held the post of comprador (a native manager of a European business house) in Jardine

Matheson & Co. for more than 50 years.

During his life, he established 47 companies by himself, with Chinese or foreign partners or with the government. It was an astonishing figure at a time when "business" was a foreign word to the vast majority of Chinese and people in commerce were regarded with disdain by the Confucian elite.

One of the first generation of entrepreneurs, he led the way for others.

Childhood

He was born on May 19, 1832 in Tangjiawan, the second son of a farming family. His father, Tang Bao-chen (唐寶臣), worked in the Morrison School. From 1842-1848 Tang Ting-shu studied at the school in Hong Kong. In exchange for his father signing a contract to work for eight years, the school charged his son no fees. It was there he acquired a fluency in English that was one of the keys to his success in life. In addition, unlike the vast majority of Chinese, he became accustomed to the presence of foreigners and interacted comfortably with them. He learnt that, as Chairman Mao put it so vividly a century later, the "Big-Noses" are paper tigers – not to be feared or loved any more than Chinese. It was these two advantages – excellent English and familiarity with foreigners – that enabled him to move easily throughout his life between the Chinese and western worlds and have friends in both.

His colleagues at Jardine, Matheson would later say that he spoke their language as well as an Englishman.

In 1862, together with his two brothers, he compiled a book "The Encyclopedia of Spoken English", using Cantonese pronunciation; it was designed to help communication between Cantonese and English speakers.

This was because the vast majority of those working with or coming into contact with the "Big-Noses" were, like Tang, from Guangdong. One section was entitled "Questions and Answers about Compradors".

It is considered the first English-Chinese dictionary and encyclopedia by a Chinese. He wrote in the preface: "When I visited offices of foreign firms in Fujian, Jiangsu and Zhejiang, people asked me many questions. Because their English was not fluent, they had lost money, been cheated or humiliated. So we publish this book to give you the correct version."

His advice is as true for Chinese today as it was in 1862.

His years at Morrison School also gave him an excellent personal network. Among his classmates was Yung Wing, the subject of our chapter one, with whom he became a lifelong friend. Many of the other graduates went on to hold important positions in the government or business.

After graduation from Morrison, he worked as an assistant in an auction house in Hong Kong. From 1851, he took a job as an interpreter in the colonial government, a post he held for seven years; from 1856, he was Chinese interpreter at the Da Shen Yuan (大審院), the court of final appeal for civil and criminal cases.

Then an Englishman he had met in the government and who had moved to the tax department of the Shanghai customs invited him to move there. He accepted the offer and worked in the customs as a senior interpreter for three years, from 1858. Shanghai was the commercial capital of China and the place to go for an ambitious young man.

Also in 1858, he took his first steps in the business world, investing in two pawnshops in Hong Kong.

In 1861, he moved to Jardine, Matheson & Co., a British firm and the leading foreign trade company in China. He received his introduction there from a clansman from Xiangshan named Lin, who was its comprador. Foreign companies like Jardine relied heavily on senior Chinese staff to deal with suppliers, wholesalers and the government; few foreign managers could speak Chinese or understood the complexities of dealing with producers of silk, tea, cotton, opium, porcelain and the other goods they wanted to buy.

This gave the compradors much space to do business on their own account and exploit the wide gap between the Chinese and the foreign worlds. Lin put Tang in charge of Jardine's gold warehouses and managing its shipping business along the Yangtze.

In 1861, Tang set up Xiuhua Cotton Company, which purchased cotton from the interior and sold it to foreign companies. It was the hottest commodity at that time. It was his first venture in foreign trade.

In 1863, he replaced Lin as the main comprador.

He worked as a comprador for Jardine for 10 years, until 1872, managing their warehouses, purchasing silk and tea and developing their shipping business in ports outside Shanghai. The most profitable lines were those to Tianjin, Xiamen, Fuzhou and Manila.

Tang managed their accounts and expanded their market share while also building a large business empire of his own. This he achieved by investing in property, transport of rice, pawnshops, salt, mining and a tea warehouse as well as in three banks in Shanghai, to help meet his need for capital.

He set up three companies in silk, tea and foreign trade; he and Xu Run (徐潤), another townsman from Tangjiawan, were both directors of the three.

Tang was a shareholder in Canton Insurance Office, which was operated by Jardine Matheson. And he was also the largest shareholder of the Huahai Steamship company, with 400 out of its 1,650 shares as well as being assistant manager and on the board. His investments included foreign companies, including Union Steam Navigation, North China Steamer and Suwonada Steamer.

He rendered great services to the foreign trading firms for whom he worked, recruiting senior staff, attracting capital and working with Chinese customers and shareholders; not to mention managing important operations and providing contacts and information.

At the same time, he himself was well rewarded and had the freedom to build up his own business portfolio. This was possible in only a few places in China; the most important was the foreign concession of Shanghai, which offered the military protection and legal and commercial conditions needed for modern business to flourish.

As a patriotic Chinese, he resented the privileges of the foreigners and the wealth they earned from them; but he too had benefited greatly, as did many of his clansmen from Tangjiawan.

One manager of Jardine Matheson said of him: "He is the guarantee by which we obtain the support of Chinese businessmen." Edward Cunningham, president of the American shipping firm, Russell & Co.（美國旗昌輪船公司）, said: "With his ability to search out information and solicit Chinese business, we are unable to compete with him." In 1877, Cunningham would sell his firm to the new company of which Tang was general manager.

Birth of China Merchants

In 1872, at the request of Li Hong-zhang, the leading economic reformer within the government, he left Jardine Matheson to prepare the establishment of China Merchants Steamship Navigation Company (CMSNC). It was a key moment in his life. After working for 21 years for foreign companies and institutions, he decided to put his skills and knowledge at the service of his government.

Friends joked that he had swapped the "leather shoes" of the foreigners for the "cloth shoes" of a Chinese official.

For the rest of his life, he became a key player in the efforts of those in the government who wanted to modernize the nation and close the enormous gap with the rich countries which had colonized it.

It would have been easier for Tang to remain a comprador; it was a steady and handsomely paid job. He could have continued his employment with Jardine and at the same time grown his personal business empire, probably becoming one of the richest people in China.

Working for Beijing, on the other hand, was a risk. As Tang well knew, the government was deeply divided between conservatives and reformers. Governance was highly personalized; policy depended on individuals in key posts. If one died or lost his position in a power struggle, everything could change – and quickly – and those who depended on his patronage could lose their positions too. It was far from the more predictable and rule-based world of international trade.

But Tang was a patriot as well as an entrepreneur. He had shown he could make his fortune in the white man's world and had seen at first hand how far China was behind Britain, France, Germany, the United States and all the countries who dominated industry and trade in Shanghai.

At Jardine, he could continue to widen this gap. Or he could take the plunge and try to narrow it, by putting his skills at the service of the state. His move was above all a bet on Li Hong-zhang, the senior official who asked him to set up CMSNC.

Self - Strengthening Movement

Li was the leader of what was known as the Self-Strengthening Movement. It was a small group of the ruling elite which believed that institutional reforms were essential after the series of military defeats which China had suffered and concessions it had been forced to make.

These reforms included the introduction of western military technology and armaments, with which Yung Wing was closely involved, as we described in chapter one. Li established arsenals in Nanjing and Tianjin in 1865 and 1867 respectively, with the help of foreign advisors and administrators. The reformers also set up shipyards in Shanghai and Fuzhou, to construct modern warships.

The conservatives in the court believed the arsenals were an enormous waste of money and that the superiority of the Chinese people rested in their moral qualities and not technological competence.

Li and the reformers argued that trade and commerce were a form of war: the foreign powers used their military power to gain commercial advantages for their companies and China should similarly favour its own firms.

In his proposal to the court for the establishment of CMSNC, he said that its vessels "should take back from foreign companies' profits and interest that should rightfully be Chinese, so that every penny we earn will be a penny less to profit a foreign enterprise". He won the argument and the government approved his proposal.

But the reformers had to act cautiously, sometimes even in secret.

To run these new companies, they needed to hire foreigners. But a majority of the ruling elite in Beijing, including Empress Dowager Cixi Taihou, hated foreigners and opposed giving them positions of responsibility in the government; they believed that these men served the interests of their own governments, not those of the Chinese state which employed them.

But the sad reality was that there was no alternative to employing these people – however expensive and arrogant they were. China did not have the skilled people who understood how to manufacture and operate steam engines, textile machinery, machine guns and battleships or how to manage international trade.

The reformers often had to conceal their plans and projects from their opponents in Beijing; it was not so difficult in a country with no newspapers or rapid means of communication. The risk was that conservative local officials would report what they had seen and heard to their masters in Beijing. The approach of the reformers is summarized in the proverb still in daily use today – "the mountain is high and the emperor is far away." What they did is copied today by many officials in China; they take initiatives they know would be opposed by their superiors and keep them secret.

By the 1870s, Li wanted to widen the scope of the reforms from the military to industry, commerce, agriculture and mining. But he knew that, if he put officials in charge of new ventures, they would fail because they had no knowledge or experience in these fields and, probably, no desire to learn.

He could not hire foreigners to head the firms. So he devised the concept of companies run by private businessmen under the supervision of the government. The capital would come from private sources; the managers would follow the policies set for them by the government, which would, if necessary, provide subsidies.

It was a "private-public partnership", not ideal but born of necessity. The modern economy of China was dominated by foreign companies, with their offices and factories in Shanghai and the other treaty ports. They had the capital, expertise, technology and market access won for them by their governments. If China were to become a modern state, it would have to create companies that could challenge these foreign firms.

Li could draw Chinese talent from the small entrepreneur class which had grown up in Hong Kong, Shanghai and other big cities; many of them, like Tang, had learnt their skills working for foreigners.

Shortly after Li had taken his post, Tang wrote to him: "In Hong Kong, we saw the foreign steamships entering our waters and earning a large profit. What we should do is establish a national shipping company, to bring the profit back home."

It was Yung Wing who had first proposed to the court in Beijing in the 1860s the idea of a national shipping line; nothing came of it until Li took office. First, he hired an official of the Zhejiang Maritime Bureau to set up the company. This he did in 1872, with the government taking 50,000 taels of stock and Li expecting the private sector to put up the rest of the capital.

The response of private companies was poor; they had no confidence in a business venture run by bureaucrats. The company had only four steamships and one pier. It lost 42,000 taels in its first six months of operation; it was not run like a modern company. This is what made Li change his plan and hire Tang, someone with a proven record in business, with an excellent network among Chinese and foreigners and access to technical expertise and private capital.

Launch of China Merchants

CMSNC was officially established on December 26, 1872 and started business on January 17 the next year in Nanshuian Street in Shanghai. Two days later, the "Aden" steamship of 507 tonnes which it had purchased for 50,000 taels from a British company left Shanghai for Hong Kong, the maiden voyage for the company.

Li asked Tang to establish and run a company that could compete with foreign firms on routes on the Yangtze River, along the coast and overseas. It was a sector with which Tang was very familiar; Li also hired Xu Run, his friend and partner from Xiangshan.

Tang took over as managing director on June 4, 1873 and did a thorough restructuring of the firm, employing Chinese managers who had worked in foreign companies and avoiding as tactfully as possible the advice sent by the Qing government. He introduced western management methods with a tight budgetary system and a lean workforce. This was a novelty in a country where bribery and overstaffing were common practice. Tang was a hands-on manager, paying close attention to detail.

Using his wide network of contacts he increased the capital fivefold from 200,000 to one million taels.

At the end of July, the Aden went to Kobe and Nagasaki on the company's first foreign voyage. It set up 19 branches, including in Tianjin, Hankou, Hong Kong, Nagasaki, Bangkok and Manila.

CMSNC succeeded in its mission to break the foreign monopoly on shipping. Its prices and services were competitive; it opened branches in Thailand and the Philippines.

In November 1875, it started an insurance company, the first by a Chinese. In December 1877, it signed agreements for the first time with the shipping companies of Swire and Jardine Matheson for common prices, an important step to make Chinese firms competitive in the market.

In 1877, it paid 2.2 million silver taels for an American shipping firm, Russell & Co., which covered the Shanghai to Tianjin and Hankou routes; its assets included seven sea and nine river vessels, smaller craft, piers and warehouses. Russell & Co. was a major shipping company and its acquisition marked the first purchase of a foreign shipping company by a Chinese firm.

Within 10 years, CMSNC had 26 boats operating on the rivers and the sea, with cargoes worth tens of thousands of taels.

In March 1878, it set up a shipping and accident insurance firm.

On October 19, 1879, one of its ships arrived in Hawaii with 400 passengers. On July 30 the next year, one ship reached San Francisco, marking the first service by a Chinese company to the North American continent.

Tang was re-appointed for a second term as general manager in January 1881 and, on October 4 that year, CMSNC's Mei Fu steamer reached Britain with a cargo of tea, the first voyage to that country.

In 1883, the company doubled its capital to two million taels, 10 times the original and making it the largest shipping company in China at that time.

During the Sino-French war (1884-85), to protect itself against being taken over by France or being used as reparations, the company signed, in July 1884, an agreement selling itself to Russell & Co. and using its flags. In May the next year, after the war was over, the company returned to CMSNC.

It broke more new ground in 1887 by setting up in Shanghai the first modern bonded warehouse in China. In 1891, it started modern China's first textile machinery factory in Shanghai.

It was one of the most successful companies set up by Li Hong-zhang and the Self-Strengthening Movement.

One well-known Shanghai businessman, Jing Yuan-shan, commented: "Tang and Xu had earned a good reputation before they entered CMSNC. Tang is so firm and persistent that no-one dealing with foreign affairs can compete with him." Jing played an important role in establishing the Shanghai Textile Bureau and Shanghai Telegraph, at the request of Li Hongzhang.

CMSNC became a model for other "public-private" partnerships in mining, telegraph, railways, banking, cotton spinning and industrial weaving.

China Merchants was one of the most successful of Li's initiatives. In 2012, it celebrated its 140th anniversary and is one of the four biggest state firms in Hong Kong.

Just as in Tang's day, it has been a pioneer in the post-1978 reform era; it set up the Shekou Industrial Zone in Shenzhen, the first open to foreign investment, the first commercial shareholding bank and insurance firm. In July 1992, it listed a transport subsidiary in Hong Kong, the first "Red Chip" (state company) on the bourse. It also has companies listed on the Shanghai and Shenzhen stock markets.

The company's principal sectors are infrastructure, ports, roads, energy, transport and logistics, financial services and real estate.

Roving diplomat

During his tenure at CMSNC, the Shanghai city government asked Tang to help with its foreign affairs; in 1877, he was appointed director of a newly established Shanghai Foreign Affairs Office.

The government wanted to accelerate the development of Taiwan and build an undersea electric cable from Fuzhou and Xiamen to the island. At that time, a Danish company was laying a cable from Fuzhou to Xiamen and the government wanted to take over the project. It sent Tang to Fuzhou to negotiate with the Danish firm. After protracted negotiations, the Chinese took over all the equipment, materials and property of the company.

He also was sent to Taiwan to settle a dispute over an accident involving a Spanish vessel. The dispute had dragged on for several years but Tang was able to settle it in eight days, earning praise from both sides.

In September 1879, he went to Yantai, Shandong to act as interpreter for Li Hong-zhang in negotiations over a treaty.

In 1879, a CMSNC ship reached Hawaii for the first time, the start of relations between China and the Kingdom.

In April 1881, the King of Hawaii paid his first visit to China; he asked for the help of China and Japan in fighting the infiltration of Britain, France, Germany and the U.S. into his country. He went to Kaiping in Hebei province to see Tang, who was working there. They talked for an entire day; they discussed how, as fellow Asians, they should combat the white race. After receiving Tang's report, Li received the King in Tianjin at a banquet and held wide-ranging talks with him.

The kingdom lasted only 12 more years. In 1893, American and European residents of Hawaii overthrew the monarchy and took over the government. They lobbied for its annexation by the U.S., which Congress approved in 1898. China could do nothing to help the king.

In 1883, on Li's instruction, Tang visited Europe to research its economy and especially the shipping business. He went to Paris, London and Amsterdam and bought an iron-clad vessel for the Chinese navy.

While he was there, the Sino-French war broke out over control over the northern half of Vietnam and he remained in Paris, to collect political and military information. During talks with the French Defence Minister, Tang discovered that the minister was pessimistic about the outcome of the war. Tang passed this information immediately to Li, telling him to continue the fight and that France would withdraw. The French government and public were ambiguous about the war.

But Li did not take his advice. The Empress Dowager was more afraid of Japan than France and ordered Li to make peace so China could focus attention on Japan. He signed a peace treaty with France in June 1885, acknowledging its control of North Vietnam. If they had followed Tang's advice, the outcome might have been different.

Another diplomatic assignment Li gave Tang was to negotiate with the Portuguese colonial government of Macao to take back a customs post at Maliuzhou (馬騮洲) which it had seized.

On one occasion, Tang was acting as interpreter for Li when he was receiving a British minister. The minister asked whether, because there were many British citizens living in Beijing, they could build a church close to the Forbidden City to hold religious services.

Angry, Li replied: "many of our citizens are living in Britain. Chinese believe in Confucianism. When you return home, please ask Queen Victoria if we could build a Confucian temple next to Buckingham Palace." When he heard this, the minister did not raise the matter again.

Kaiping coal mine

In 1876, Li entrusted Tang with another strategic mission – the first large-scale modern coal mine operated by a Chinese company. This was the Kaiping Coal Mine in Tangshan, Hebei province. The supply of energy was critical for the development of the military and modern industry. Coal was essential to drive steam engines.

At that time, China largely depended on foreign coal; imports of coal and steel cost the government six-seven million taels a year.

Tang wrote to Li: "China itself does not have enough to use, so why do we allow others to tap our mineral wealth?" In 1876, Tang heard that residents of Kaiping township were digging for coal; he took a boat there to see for himself. After conducting his own investigation, he wrote to Li, proposing that they establish a coal mine and steel factory there.

Sceptical of a fellow Chinese, Li appointed an English engineer to do a complete geological survey and calculate the value of the reserves.

When he received a positive report, he was persuaded to go ahead with the project and appointed Tang as managing director. Tang appointed his close friend and associate Xu Run to take over the management of CMSNC and moved to Tianjin, where the mine had its headquarters.

It was a shareholding company, in which CMSNC took a stake.

This was the project to which Tang devoted the most time during his life, from the initial geological surveys, planning and raising capital until the start of production. He used his many contacts to raise one million taels in capital and used the money to import all the machinery and equipment from abroad.

The first two shafts were sunk in 1879, to a depth of 600 feet, by the new Chinese Engineering and Mining Company, under the direction of English mining engineer Robert Reginald Burnett; production began in 1881.

Tang hired three other foreign engineers and 14 Europeans as managers of other parts of the operation. In addition, he hired 50 mining technicians from Guangdong, including one of his own sons who had studied mining in the U.S.. He hired 3,000 workers to work the coal face and do other jobs.

In 1884, he introduced a bonus system which awarded more to those who mined more. He regularly went to the coal face himself to inspect the work and when he saw workers who were sick, he ordered them to rest and not go down the mine.

By the end of the 19th century, it had an annual output of more than 700,000 tonnes, the largest of any state mine; its capital had increased five-fold to five million taels. Between 1889 and 1899, it made profits of five million taels. It was the most successful coal mine operated by the government. Many attributed this to Tang himself, saying that China did not have another manager of his calibre.

The mine lives on today as the Kailuan Coal Group, one of the largest coal-producers in the country.

Building a Railway

During his initial inspection, Tang realized that transporting the coal was as important as mining it. So he proposed to Li construction of a railway to run 65 kilometres to Tianjin, one of China's biggest ports.

But, at that time, building a railway was highly controversial. In 1876, a British businessman had laid the country's first line, the Wusong railway, on the outskirts of Shanghai. Strongly opposed to the idea, the government bought it at a high price, dismantled it and shipped the rails to Taiwan.

Many at the court, including the Empress Dowager, believed that steam engines disturbed the spirits of their ancestors and dragons below the ground and that this would have terrible consequences.

It proposed to Tang that, instead, he build a canal to carry the coal. He replied that the terrain did not permit this; so the government compromised, saying that he could build a railway but use donkeys, not steam engines.

By 1881, the company had finished a line of 11 km from Tangshan to Xugezhuang, under the direction of British civil engineer Claude William Kinder. He built it to the international standard gauge of 1,435 mm so that it could be turned into a full railway. It was called the Tang-Xu (唐胥) line.

In accordance with Beijing's instructions, donkeys pulled the coal carts. When the foreign employees saw this, they laughed in scorn and ridicule. They asked: was this how China was going to become a modern state and produce steel and warships?

Tang agreed with his foreign colleagues and decided to disobey the orders of Beijing. He accepted a proposal from Kinder to build a steam engine and used scrap metal from the mine to build a 100-ton engine, "the Rocket of China" which was completed in 1881. They had to complete the project in complete secrecy.

The engine began operations on June 9, 1881. It was a historic moment – a Chinese-made steam engine was pulling coal on the country's first standard-gauge railway. The news soon reached the palace, where there was uproar. It issued an order banning the steam engine, saying that its movements and black smoke were disturbing the imperial ancestors in their tombs.

But Tang was insistent; he could not go back to donkeys. He knew he had the backing of Li Hong-zhang and the reformists in the court; he would not back down. Finally, the court lifted the ban.

In 1882, Tang ordered two more locomotives from manufacturer Robert Stephenson & Co. of Newcastle. They arrived in October that year and were given the numbers two and three. They were the first two standard gauge locomotives imported into China.

Opposition from the court prevented extension of the railway for several years. But, because the canal was frozen with ice for several months in winter, Tang in 1886 succeeded in gaining permission to extend it to Lutai, a town with a river, on which boats could carry the coal.

This was done by a new company, Kaiping Railway Company, which was separately funded from the mining firm. Its chairman was Zhou Fu (周馥), the official in charge of Tianjin, and managing director Wu Ting-fang (伍廷芳), who had studied law in England and was secretary and interpreter to Li Hong-zhang.

Diversification

Tang also established China's first modern cement factory in Tangshan. While this was already being used as a construction material, there was no word for it in Chinese. So the name of the firm was Tangshan Ximiantu (細綿土) Factory. Later a word was coined that has become the standard usage – 水泥 (shuini, which means "water mud").

The success of the Kaiping Coal Mine and the substantial profits it generated were important for the reformers in the government; they were an example of how their projects were yielding benefit to the country and giving employment to its people.

The Kaiping coal won the Tianjin market and displaced imported coal. It gave the reformers money to spend on coastal defence as well as a good return to the initial investors.

Tianjin was a showcase city of Li's reforms. He built there a large arsenal and an academy to train military officers; he also built port facilities as well as a railway network connecting it to neighbouring cities and mines.

During his years in the government, Tang had a senior high rank. But he was not comfortable with the lifestyle and trappings of officialdom. He despised the scheming of the court and the widespread bribery and malpractice. He rarely wore the ornate robes of an official, preferring a western business suit. He saw himself as a businessman working for the government, rather than a civil servant. He was interested in achieving actual results and not the prestige and privileges of a high official.

Li had enormous confidence in him. He used to say: "China could do without Li Hong-zhang, but not without Tang Ting-shu."

He also continued to invest on his own behalf; he put HK$100,000 into a shipping company in Hong Kong, which leased two vessels for the Hong Kong-Shanghai route. He and Xu Run rented two warehouses on the Shanghai docks and established two insurance companies, Renhe and Jihe; they were the first insurance firms set up by a Chinese. Previously, the business was monopolized by foreign companies. Many regard him as the father of China's insurance industry.

In 1883, with another businessman Li Wen-hao, he established the Chengping silver mine in Rehe province, also known as Jehol, in north China. In 1887 and 1888, he and Xu Run set up the Pingquan copper mine and Qianan Steel factory.

These projects were part of a wider plan of Li Hong-zhang, who wanted to create a modern industrial base in China.

In May 1874, he gave financial support to Hui Bao in Shanghai, only the second newspaper set up by a Chinese – his former classmate Yung Wing.

Yung believed that newspapers in Shanghai were biased and inaccurate and decided to set up a new one. The first Chinese newspaper had been founded in Hong Kong six months earlier.

Passing

Tang died on October 7, 1892, while working at the Kaiping Coal mine headquarters in Tianjin; he was just 60. He probably died of an infectious disease that was sweeping the city.

In its obituary, the North China Herald, a Shanghai newspaper, said that he represented an era in Chinese history. "His death is a great loss to the Chinese and the foreign community ... he will be very hard to replace." Nearly 1,000 people attended his funeral; public buildings and the 13 foreign consulates in the city flew their flags at half-mast.

The CMSNC provided a boat to take his body back to his town. In a mark of tribute to him, the foreign consulates and trading firms provided 13 boats to see him off from Tianjin and escort him all the way home.

The cortege stopped on the Huangpu River in Shanghai, where 1,100 people came to say their farewells. All the lights on The Bund were lit up. Then the fleet proceeded to Tangjiawan for burial, escorted by the 13 ships, their flags all at half-mast. The foreign representatives threw wreaths of flowers from the shore.

CMSNC named one of its ships Ting-shu in his honour.

Wealth and philanthropy

During his career, Tang amassed a personal fortune estimated at more than one million taels, an enormous sum at that time. What happened to all this money is something of a mystery.

Much was invested in companies that were part state and part private; some made no profit, others lost money.

He was an active philanthropist. The six-volume Chinese-English dictionary he wrote in 1862 he printed and sold at his own expense. He wrote it in response to the many questions he was asked during his work at Jardines.

It includes a list of English and Chinese words arranged by different kinds of transactions, including metals, tobacco, silk, tea, fabric, weights, measurements, accounts, rules governing lawsuits, personnel, shipping, hiring, currency and warehousing. It also contains dialogues for use in negotiations.

He wrote the translations of English words with the pronunciation in Cantonese – a sign of the importance of this community in dealing with the foreigners.

In 1870, he and Xu Run spent heavily to set up the Renji Hospital (仁濟醫院) in Shanghai. That year, he also donated funds for a distribution of food to the city's poor conducted by its churches.

In 1872, he and Xu Run founded the Guangzhao (廣肇公所) Association in Shanghai and provided a room for it to hold meetings The name combined "Guang" from Guangzhou and "Zhao" from Zhaoxing. It became a rendezvous place for the many Cantonese people in Shanghai. At its inaugural dinner, it collected more than 10,000 taels from the participants.

In 1874, he supported an initiative of the British consul in Shanghai to set up an English reading room; of the three directors, he was the only Chinese. That year he also supported the Anglo-Chinese School, for the children of Chinese business people.

In 1882, in Tangshan, he set up nine free schools for the children of poor workers. His other philanthropic projects there included an irrigation and animal husbandry company in Tanggu, which used machinery to develop idle land. He allowed local people to open small mines. When he was 60, the people of 48 mining districts nearby gave him a gift of an umbrella (萬民牌傘), in thanks and congratulation.

He gave financial support to the first newspaper founded in Shanghai by a Chinese, his ex-classmate Yung Wing, in May 1874. He also played an important role in Yung's project to send 120 Chinese students to the U.S..

Yung could find no parents willing to send their children; they feared that they would become Americans and never return to China. Tang supported this initiative and returned to Tangjiawan to ask families there to let their sons go; he persuaded at least five.

In Tangjiawan, he funded the construction of a pier from where ships would go to Guangzhou and Hong Kong. He also paid for a clinic for the poor, a free school and a hospital. After his death, the school and clinic closed for lack of funds.

He led a family of entrepreneurs. His brother and two other relatives followed him as comprador of Jardine; the Tang family held the post for half a century. A younger brother served as manager of CMSNC's Shanghai, Guangdong and Fuzhou offices and a cousin was a senior manager at the Hong Kong and Shanghai Bank.

He had nine children, many of whom went into business. The family is now scattered across the world, in Hong Kong, Macao and the U.S.

Legacy

Many of Tang's projects exist and are thriving today. The Renji Hospital in Shanghai has become the Number Three People's Hospital and continues to offer western and Chinese medicine.

The pier in Tangjiawan was mentioned in Sun Yat-sen's famous book on national development strategy ("The International Development of China"), in which he called it Tang Jia Da Gang (the big port of Tangjia). But it was destroyed during the Japanese occupation of the township.

Tang's greatest legacy today is two companies, China Merchants Group and the Kaiping Coal Mine, which has become the Kailuan Group. Both have grown into conglomerates and major firms in their fields.

China Merchants Bank is one of the most successful of the shareholding banks set up during the reform era. It is the sixth largest commercial bank in China in terms of total assets. In 2009, it acquired full ownership of Wing Lung, a private bank in Hong Kong, and has offices in New York, London and Taipei.

What would please Tang the most is how CMB is part of China's economic independence. To mine coal and build railway lines to carry it to clients, Tang had no alternative but to employ expensive foreigners who had knowledge and experience that did not exist in China at that time.

When he ran CMG, its main competitors even on routes within China were foreign shipping companies that used the privileges won for them by their governments and the finance provided by their banks. They controlled the export markets where Chinese goods were sold. They had expertise and management systems unknown to Chinese.

Tang introduced this expertise and management into CMG and made it competitive with the foreign firms. If he saw it today, he would see a company that can import and export the goods China needs and more than compete with foreign firms; it is taking market share from them.

He would also be happy at its diversification into many sectors. He was an entrepreneur who also invested broadly and was not afraid to take a new challenge. The political and financial conditions in which he operated were so much more difficult than those of CMG in the 21st century. They make his achievements the more remarkable.

China has become the world's biggest producer and consumer of coal, with output in 2012 of 3.65 billion tones, up 3.7 per cent on 2011. It accounts for 80 per cent of the fuel used to generate electricity.

The coal operation that Tang founded in Kaiping has played an important role. It is strategically placed close to Beijing and Tianjin, two of the country's most important industrial cities, and has railway connections to the ports of Tianjin and Qinhuangdao, from which the coal is shipped to south China.

When Tang and his foreign employees were watching the donkeys pull the coal carts, none of them could have imagined such an outcome.

The six-volume Chinese-English dictionary written by Tang Ting-shu in 1862.

Pages from the dictionary of Tang Ting-shu.

A brick-making machine in the Kaiping coal mine.

The railway line at the Kaiping coal mine.

Chapter Four

徐潤
1838 - 1911

Dealmaker Extraordinary

Xu Run

Introduction

The name of Xu Run is closely linked to that of Tang Ting-shu. The two sons of Xiangshan worked together on many projects, including China Merchants Steamship Navigation Company (CMSNC), the Kaiping coal mine and China's first insurance company. They had a similar profile – they worked for more than 10 years as compradors for a foreign trading company before setting up on their own and then managing government-backed projects. Both were pioneers in creating a modern business culture in China.

Both became very wealthy. Xu was the richer of the two and one of the wealthiest people in China. He amassed a large part of his fortune from the property market in Shanghai and also invested in Guangzhou, Tianjin, Beidaihe and other cities. He set up a company that became China's largest exporter of tea. He built a house in Shanghai's international concession that was so large that visitors got lost when they entered it. It was immaculately maintained by an army of servants who kept the floors and desks "shining as glass". He sent his children and grandchildren to study in Oxford and the United States.

He also established the country's first private modern printing company which published Chinese classics and translations of English books. He was a generous philanthropist, giving to famine relief, schools, hospitals and the Red Cross.

But his reputation was tarnished by a scandal – in 1884, he appropriated money from CMSNC to speculate in the Shanghai property market; it turned against him. Although he repaid all the money he had taken, he had to resign from the company and the government never had the same trust in him.

Born into a comprador family

Xu was born on December 14, 1838 in Beiling (北嶺) village in Xiangshan. His family was higher up the social ladder than that of Tang; one relative had been a government official and his uncle, Xu Rong-cun (徐榮村) was a comprador with Dent & Co. (寶順洋行), a British trading firm. He spent his early years in Beiling, studying with teachers hired by his family.

In 1852, at the age of 14, he went with uncle Rong-cun via Macao to Shanghai. After a brief period of study in Suzhou, he returned to Shanghai and, thanks to the introduction of his uncle, entered Dent & Co. as an apprentice, still aged 14; he would work there for 16 years.

His uncle had become famous for shipping 12 bales of Chinese silk to the Great Exhibition in the Crystal Palace, London in 1851. It was the first of a series of World Fairs in the second half of the 19th century. Opened by Queen Victoria, the event was an opportunity for Great Britain to show its industrial and manufacturing leadership in many fields. More than a dozen countries took part. Xu's uncle's entry was not well wrapped or presented but the fine quality of the silk attracted the attention of the judges and won a gold medal. With this recognition and the praise of the Queen herself, his goods were in future able to enter the British market without paying duty. Xu's uncle was the first Chinese to display goods at an international exhibition and his was one of the first Chinese brands.

Dent's was one of the wealthiest British merchant firms during the 19th century and a rival to Jardine, Matheson, where Tang Ting-shu worked. Thomas Dent arrived in Guangzhou in 1823 and joined a trading company; the next year, he changed the name to Dent & Co.. In 1839, Lin Ze-xu (林則徐), the official charged by the government with eliminating the opium trade, issued a warrant for Dent's arrest and forced him to hand over his store of opium; it was the opening shot of the First Opium War (see chapter one). In 1841, Dent moved its headquarters to what is now the Central district of Hong Kong. In 1843, he was one of the first merchants to set up an office in Shanghai, at 14 The Bund, after it opened to foreign trade. He was a founding member of the committee that established the Hong Kong & Shanghai Bank in March 1865.

When Xu joined, the company's main business was importing cloth, pharmaceuticals and mixed cargo and exporting silk, cotton and tea; it had its own fleet of ships. Xu was intelligent and hard-working and quickly learnt the intricacies of foreign trade, including a mastery of English.

In the diary he wrote later in life, he remembered his feelings on arrival in Shanghai: "The foreigners are not content with what they have and Japan is seeking to expand. The government has no policy and gives up the land easily. When a person is poor, he thinks of himself. When he is rich, he thinks of others."

In 1856, he became an assistant accountant at Dent, then a chief accountant and, in 1861, assistant comprador. He then took over as chief comprador when the incumbent became unable to continue because of excessive drinking.

Xu also went into business on his own account. In 1859, with two Chinese associates, he started a company named Shaoxiang (紹祥), which purchased silk, tea and cotton in the interior and sold it to foreign firms in Shanghai for a profit. With others, he also invested in a private bank, Dun Mao (敦茂).

Business opportunities for Dent and the other foreign firms greatly increased after the Second Opium War of 1856-1860 and the treaties which China was forced to sign after its defeat. Under the Treaty of Tianjin of 1858 (which ended the first part of that war), Beijing opened 10 more ports to foreign trade and gave foreign vessels the right to navigate freely on the Yangtze River. It also allowed foreigners the right to travel in the internal regions of China for the first time.

Xu established branches in Yantai, Tianjin, Zhenjiang, Wuhu, Jiujiang and Hankou, added to those in Hong Kong and Shanghai, which was its headquarters. He extended the firm's trading business to Kobe, Nagasaki and Yokohama in Japan and purchased docks and ships. Dent's fleet had a total of 10 vessels, including river and ocean ships. This was the golden period of Dent, with its import and export value exceeding 10 million taels a year. As the general comprador, Xu received a commission of three per cent. This enabled Xu to become extremely wealthy and gain invaluable experience in foreign trade.

At the same time, his own private business expanded. Between 1859 and 1864, he invested in property in Shanghai, private banks in Wenzhou, Ningbo and Hankou, exported tea and silk and imported opium.

The Second Opium War and the treaties which the government was forced to sign had a profound impact on China. The imperial army was defeated by an Anglo-French military force one tenth of its size. The Europeans burnt to the ground the Summer Palace in Beijing, one of the architectural marvels of the world, and the Emperor fled from the capital.

It was a humiliation for a country that had long considered itself the centre of the world. But out of this tragedy came something positive; a group of high officials, led by Zeng Guo-fan, Li Hong-zhang Zhang Zhi-dong (張之洞) and Zuo Zong-tang (左宗棠) decided that, if things did not change, China would become a colony of the foreign powers. They launched what became known as the Self-Strengthening Movement that aimed to introduce major reforms and modernize the country. The sons of Xiangshan, including Tang and Xu, would play an important role in this movement.

Then, suddenly, Dent's golden summer came to an abrupt end. In 1867, a discount house in London collapsed causing a run on many banks which in turn brought down other businesses. Jardines averted disaster by learning the news sooner – its mail steamer carrying news from Calcutta arrived one hour earlier than others – and emptying its balances at a failing bank before anyone else in Hong Kong had heard the news. But Dent did not escape – it was forced to close its operations in Hong Kong.

In 1868, Xu left the company. His 16 years there had brought him a substantial fortune and invaluable professional experience. But, according to Chinese scholars, the relationship between a comprador and his foreign bosses was far from equal. Both were essential to the smooth running of the company – the comprador dealt with the "Chinese world", organizing the supply of goods from local companies and managing local employees, while the "Big-Noses" dealt with the "foreign world", including buyers in the west, banks to provide financing and insurance firms to provide coverage. China was a feudal society with a rigid hierarchy. British and other Europeans who managed the foreign firms were like mandarins in the government and the compradors served them like junior officials. From their foreign bosses, Xu and Tang earned money and valuable experience but not equality or status.

As he started the next chapter of his professional life, Xu could scarcely have been better placed – he had rich experience in foreign trade, knowledge of Chinese and foreign ports, a wide network of contacts across the country and a substantial personal fortune.

He set up the Bao Yuan Xiang (寶源祥) Tea Company, with branches in Zhejiang, Jiangxi, Hubei and Hunan provinces. He understood the domestic market and knew consumer tastes in Britain, America, Russia and other countries. He and Tang Ting-shu set up the Shanghai Tea Centre, which controlled the tea trade in Shanghai and surrounding areas. Tea was one of China's four most important exports.

The 20 years between 1868 and 1888 were the golden period for tea exports; in 1886, the volume was 134,000 tonnes, a seven-fold increase from 1846 and accounting for 62 per cent of all China's exports. It was a record that was not broken until 1986.

This rapid increase in exports was both good and bad news for China. The signing of the treaties after the Opium Wars had opened ports to foreign trade; fast, modern vessels were able to deliver increasing amounts of tea to markets in the west where demand was rising. But this improvement in sea transport also brought an increase in imports of opium.

So China was obliged to increase its exports of tea – and silk – to pay for vast amounts of opium. Shanghai's tea exports accounted for two thirds of that of the whole country and Bao Yuan Xiang was the largest tea exporting company. Xu earned the name of "king of modern China's tea exports". His companies handled other commodities, including silk, hemp, cotton tobacco and tung oil.

Over the next 20 years, Xu became one of the most prominent Guangdong entrepreneurs in Shanghai. His most profitable investment was real estate. He was one of the earliest to see the potential of Shanghai after the Second Opium War as the industrial, commercial and trading centre of China so he invested heavily in buying land in the prime areas, mostly financed by loans from banks on his own property.

In association with foreign and Chinese partners, he set up five real estate companies. Once he had developed a site, he borrowed against it to finance new purchases. By 1884, he had invested more than two million taels of silver in real estate on a total of 3,000 mu (200 hectares) of land; on them, he built houses, 50 apartment buildings and 2,000 shops. He also bought land and built houses in other cities like Tianjin, Tanggu, Guangzhou, Zhenjiang and Beidaihe.

Chinese scholars estimate that he earned annual rents of more than 120,000 taels, with the properties outside Shanghai worth over one million taels. They put his personal worth at 3.41 million taels, of which property accounted for 2.23 million, stocks 800,000 and pawnshops and banks 340,000.

In 1869, the Suez Canal opened to shipping and in 1871, the laying of undersea cables enabled Shanghai and London to be connected by telegram. The pace of international trade was accelerating.

Shipping company

From 1873, Xu changed the focus of his life in the same way as Tang Ting-shu, his friend and fellow son of Xiangshan. The two men were closely involved in the foundation of the China Merchants Steamship Navigation Company (CMSNC), which we described in the previous chapter.

Tang was general director and hired Xu as deputy director, with a salary of several thousand taels a year. Xu invested 240,000 taels of his own money, accounting for nearly 25 per cent of the share capital. In 1884, when Tang increased the share capital, Xu subscribed more than anyone else, doubling his investment to 480,000 taels. When Tang went to set up Kaiping Coal Mining in 1876, Xu took over day-to-day management of the CMSNC.

Xu played an important role in the acquisition of the American shipping firm, Russell & Co.. When Xu heard the news of its financial troubles, Tang was in Fuzhou on business and out of contact; Xu had to make the decision on his own – he chose to purchase the company. The purchase was both an important step to expand the company and a symbol that it could compete successfully with foreign lines.

CMSNC became a major national company, with more than 20 departments. Tang and Xu ran it as a modern firm; when they could not find qualified Chinese people, they hired foreigners, especially those with technical skills and strong management ability and as captains of ships, with Chinese serving as their deputies. By 1881, it had 26 ships, up from the initial four, with berths and warehouses in 26 ports, including Yokohama, Kobe, Singapore, Malaysia, Vietnam and Philippines, up from the initial two. It was a fiercely competitive market, in which the foreign lines had early-mover advantage and the benefits bestowed on them by the unequal treaties.

Insurance pioneers

Xu and Tang were also pioneers in China's insurance industry. Before 1875, this sector was monopolized by foreign insurers. When Xu sought coverage for "Eden", CMSNC's first vessel, the foreign firms refused on the grounds that it was a Chinese ship flying the Chinese flag and they had no confidence in such a combination. After tough negotiations, one foreign company agreed to provide coverage but with strict conditions and at a high cost.

In April 1875, Fu Sheng (福生), a ship of CMSNC, was hit by Ao Shun (奧順), a ship chartered by Jardine's, and sank; it was carrying a cargo of rice and wine, 65 passengers and 53 Chinese and foreign crew. A total of 23 people drowned and cargo worth 100,000 taels was lost. The Shanghai government and British consul ordered compensation but the owner ran away and payment was delayed.

These events made Xu and Tang determined to set up their own company. In 1876, Xu, Tang and two associates put up 250,000 taels (500,000 taels) to establish the Renhe Maritime Insurance Company (仁和水險公司), managed by CMSNC. It was China's first insurance company and provided services to ships and goods of CMSNC as well as foreign goods. Shortly afterwards, they set up the Jihe Flood and Fire Insurance Company (濟和水火險公司), with shares worth 500,000 taels, to provide coverage for ships operating on inland rivers. From 1879 to 1883, seven of the firm's ships were lost. Without insurance, the losses to the company would have been very severe. In 1886, the two companies were merged to form Renjihe Insurance Company (仁濟和保險公司). It was a successful firm, with the capital reaching five million taels, and provided coverage for both CMSNC and other Chinese firms and competition for foreign companies in the sector.

These companies were the forerunners of China's insurance industry.

Like Tang, Xu was a strong supporter of the Self-Strengthening Movement and invested his money as well as his time and energy in the companies which were set up because of it. Between 1861 and 1868, he invested a total of 1.275 million taels in different companies set up at the behest of the state.

Disgrace

In 1883-84, Shanghai was hit by a financial crisis. This was due in part to a stagnant silk market and speculative demand for shares in joint-stock companies. Their failure led to a drop in the value of real estate and commodities, which had commonly been used as security for loans. Another factor was the Sino-French war which broke out in 1883. The French attacked Taiwan and Fujian, causing panic in Shanghai and making people rush to withdraw their money from banks.

The crisis left Xu exposed. He had borrowed heavily to finance the expansion of his businesses, using land and shares as collateral. Suddenly, these assets were worth substantially less than they had been and he had large debt payments to make. To meet these, he appropriated money from CMSNC. It was common practice among Chinese entrepreneurs to mix their own and their company finances and repay the money when they could. But CMSNC was not Xu's private company, it was a national firm established by the highest leaders of the state. When Li Hong-zhang was told of the appropriations, he was very angry and ordered an aide and confidant, Sheng Xuan-huai to investigate.

Unfortunately for Xu, he and Sheng were bitter personal enemies; both were involved in CMSNC. After the details of Xu's appropriation become clear, he was forced to resign from the company and his reputation was badly tarnished. While such behaviour was common among the owners of private companies, it could not be forgiven in such a rich and prominent business leader. Xu never again enjoyed the same trust and confidence of Li Hong-zhang.

Recovery

The next six years were the most difficult of his life. His reputation was damaged and he was forced to leave the company with which he had been closely associated for 10 years. His tea business and other ventures went into the red.

However, by 1890, he had repaid to CMSNC the money he had appropriated and he decided to take new directions in life.

One such move was the foundation of China's first privately owned modern printing plant. This was the Tongwen Publishing House (同文書局) which he set up in Shanghai in 1882. He imported from Britain 12 rotary press machines and employed 500 people. It specialized in printing Chinese classics, as well as translation of English books, and published a total of more than 200,000 volumes. They were of good quality and had a big impact on society; it helped to preserve China's cultural heritage. Li Hong-zhang praised its selection of high-quality foreign books and for helping to spread new ideas from home and abroad. Unfortunately, a big fire ravaged the plant in 1892; due to financial troubles and fierce competition, it closed in 1898.

The second new direction Xu took, like Tang Ting-shu, was to develop the mineral wealth of China. He invested 150,000 taels in the Kaiping coal mine which Tang established. Over the next more than 10 years, he travelled widely to take part in the development of coal, gold and silver mines in Anhui, Hebei and Liaoning. This journey took him to places he had never seen before, a world far from the wealth and comfort in which he lived in Shanghai, allowing him to see the harsh living conditions and grinding poverty in which the mining communities lived. He was, like Tang, a pioneer in China's mining industry. The time he spent in these cold climates in the north worsened a lung illness from which he had suffered since middle age. He paid little attention to it and suffered from an increasingly severe cough.

His last business venture was the Jing Lun Shirt and Trouser factory in Shanghai which a relative had set up, but without success. He took over the management in 1908 and turned it into a leader in its field, selling its products in China and Southeast Asia. After Xu died, a grandson took it over and ran it until he was more than 80.

By now, his health was deteriorating. He spent an increasing amount of time at his spacious villa he had built in the Bubbling Well Road (靜安寺路) in the international concession in Shanghai. There he wrote his memories and notes about life in Shanghai. In 1910, he returned to his native village of Beiling in Xiangshan and ordered the construction of Yu Yuan (愚園), a large garden in the Suzhou style with paintings and sculptures. Later it fell into ruin.

He died at his home in Shanghai on March 9, 1911, at the age of 73. A cortege carrying his coffin went by sea from Shanghai via Macao to Beiling village for burial in a local cemetery. During the Cultural Revolution, people broke the grave and opened the coffin, finding only clothes inside; perhaps the body had been buried in Shanghai.

Philanthropist

During his later life, he was an enthusiastic philanthropist, involved in the establishment of the Renji Hospital and Gezhi (格致) Academy in Shanghai, Chinese Red Cross and other institutions. In 1894, in response to a famine in Tangshan, he organized a collection of 300,000 taels to buy relief goods. With Tang Ting-shu, he established the Guangzhao (廣肇) society in Shanghai as a meeting place for the city's Cantonese residents. He also provided 3,000 taels for construction of a Guangdong Building in Tianjin organized by Tang Shao-yi.

He gave 3,000 taels toward construction of a school in his native Beiling.

In 1881, he helped the Chinese students who had abruptly been ordered back from the U.S. after the end of the mission organized by Yung Wing.

They arrived in Shanghai, where they knew no-one and were coldly treated. Xu gave each of them 30-50 silver dollars and helped them to find jobs in government departments and companies, ranging from telegraph and railway to shipping and the mining industry.

The headquarters of China Merchants Steamship Navigation Company (CMSNC) in Shanghai.

A vessel of China Merchants Steamship Navigation Company.

Chapter Five

1862 - 1938

Conscience of Politics

唐紹儀

Tang Shao-yi

Introduction

Among the 12 sons of Xiangshan featured in this book, Tang Shao-yi is the best known – he was the first Prime Minister of the Republic of China and played a key role in the negotiations to end the Qing dynasty without bloodshed. He was also the diplomat who persuaded the British government to recognize Chinese sovereignty over Tibet after it had sent an army to conquer the territory. He was also a model chief of his native county. These were significant achievements.

He was one of the 120 young men to study in the United States, including a year at Columbia University. After his return to China in 1881, he held senior positions in the Qing government and was one of the most important advisors to Yuan Shi-kai (袁世凱) . But his sympathies were closer to those of the revolutionaries who were trying to bring down the government, many of them from his native Guangdong province. So it was that he became the first Premier of the new republic.

From the time he resigned the post in 1912 until his death in 1938, he was a senior figure in the Nationalist party (國民黨) but did not play a major role in government; he was too liberal, a man who had embraced the ideals of the system he had seen during his seven years in the U.S. and believed that they should be implemented at home. But China was not ready for these ideals. After the revolution of 1911, the country was controlled by generals and warlords; power came from the barrel of a gun. Tang had no soldiers – and remained a marginal figure.

For five years, he was chief of Xiangshan county, then re-named Zhongshan in honour of Dr. Sun Yat-sen (who was also known as Sun Zhong-shan). He was a model chief who worked at the grass roots, introducing buses and modern drainage that brought running water to the homes. He refused the bribes that were routinely offered to people in his position and paid for many of the improvements out of his own pocket.

Tang was a friend and adviser of Dr. Sun Yat-sen and many others at the top of public life. He entertained them at the spacious estate he built in his hometown, an estate he bequeathed to the citizens of the township and which is open now to visitors, who can enjoy the dozens of species of trees he brought from all over Asia.

Early life and education

Unlike many members of the China Educational Mission, Tang Shao-yi was born into a prosperous family. He was the fourth of six sons of Tang Yong-da (唐永大, also known as Tang Ju-chuan 唐巨川), a tea exporter in Shanghai. Tang Yong-da had gone to the city with Tang Ting-shu, a relative, who helped him to establish his business; the family was middle class, not rich. They came from Tangjiawan, where Tang was born on January 2, 1862. When he was nine, he went to join his father in Shanghai, where he went to a missionary school. There he acquired an early knowledge of English; he also studied Chinese classics and was an excellent student. He caught the eye of Tang Ting-shu, who liked him and wanted him to further his education; he proposed that the young man become one of the students sent to the U.S..

"At that time, rich Chinese would never send their children abroad to study," said Tang Jing-tan (唐景曇), a grandson of Tang Shao-yi, in an interview in one of his former homes in Tangjiawan. "It was the poor who went abroad, in search of a better life. But Shao-yi's mother was strongly in favour of the idea. She had heard from Ting-shu how the Chinese in Hong Kong and Macao were exploited and bullied because they could not speak English. She realized that it was an important tool. For his part, his father had no objection and Shao-yi himself was willing to go."

So, in 1874, he joined the third group of Chinese students sent to the U.S., going with another boy from his hometown. He first lived with the family of Eugene Gardner in Springfield, Massachusetts, where he completed his primary education at Hooker Grammar School. Then he moved to Hartford Public High School in Connecticut, where he lived with another American family. "These families looked after him very well," said Tang Jing-tan. "They treated him like one of their own family. They had no prejudice." They wanted him to convert to Christianity but did not put pressure on him.

He adapted quickly to American life; he made friends with Americans and other foreign students. Like other Chinese students, he was embarrassed by the pigtail that subjects of the Emperor were required to wear; so he cut it off. But, when he met Chinese officials in the U.S. and after he returned to China, he used a fake one; sometimes it fell off – fortunately, no-one reported him for this serious sign of disloyalty.

After graduating with honours, he enrolled in Columbia University in New York City and studied liberal arts. But he had completed only one year when the Qing government recalled the mission in 1881. Tang spent seven years in the U.S. and they had a profound impact on him as he became fluent in English and knowledgeable about American society and ways of thinking. He was at ease with the members of the American elite who were his fellow students. This gave him the self-confidence and skills to befriend and negotiate with foreigners – an important part of his life and work after he returned to China.

He also became convinced of the merits of the society he saw in the U.S. and sought to introduce them into in his home country. This was a critical factor 30 years later when he was chosen to represent the central government in negotiations with the revolutionaries who had overthrown the Qing dynasty. He was in sympathy with them; this made an agreement easy to reach.

Meets his patron: a decade in Korea

On his return to China in 1881, Tang was, with the other students, held in confinement in a college in Shanghai for six months. Alarmed that they had been westernized, the government insisted that they undergo half a year of re-education "to become Chinese again". Tang was then sent to study at the Naval School in Tianjin and, in 1885, went to work as a translator at the tax bureau in the city.

It was in Tianjin that he had his first big break – he made the acquaintance of Yuan Shi-kai, one of the most powerful military officials in the last two decades of Qing rule. Beijing had sent Yuan to Seoul to train 500 Korean soldiers in modern warfare, to defend the country against Japan. In 1885, Yuan was appointed Imperial Resident of Seoul, the equivalent of ambassador. He was also the top adviser to the Korean government. It was a period of chaos and uncertainty. China and Japan were fighting for control of the country; each had supporters within the court and the government. China was its traditional patron, while Japan saw an opportunity to replace China using its new modern army and navy.

In April 1885, China and Japan signed the *Tianjin Convention*, under which each agreed not to send troops to Korea without informing the other. Tang met Yuan at the signing; the two men took to each other and became firm friends. Yuan admired the polish and sophistication of this young man who had studied at Columbia University and could speak foreign languages; he himself had twice failed the imperial examination and entered the government through the purchase of a minor post. Then he used his father's connections to become an officer in the army; it was through the army that he rose in the government.

In his private life, he was a typical high official – he had 10 wives and concubines and 32 children. For his part, Tang badly needed a patron if he was to have a future in the Qing government. Seven years in the

U.S. was not a good preparation for an official career, especially after the government had cancelled the student mission. Many civil servants were conservative and xenophobic; they regarded the returnees with suspicion, as no longer "pure" Chinese but "half-American", full of bizarre ideas and theories that had no place in the imperial kingdom. Yuan's backing and patronage enabled Tang, then only 23, to hold important posts first in Korea and then in China; it was the springboard for his career.

"Yuan liked my grandfather for several reasons," said Jing-tan. "He saw that he was capable, efficient and understood English. It was good for him to have such a capable assistant. Another reason was an incident in which armed soldiers came to the royal palace (in Seoul), where the king and Yuan were. Tang stood in front of the palace and drove them away. The two men respected each other. To attain and keep the high positions he did, Yuan was not a simple character. Yuan advocated the modernization of China and my grandfather supported him in this."

In 1889, Yuan appointed Tang to manage China's commercial and political interests at Inchon, the main port of Seoul. He served as Yuan's chief diplomatic consultant and took charge of Chinese affairs in Korea in 1894, when Yuan went to Beijing on the eve of the Sino-Japanese War of 1894-95.

This turned out to be a godsend for Yuan, since he was not directly involved in the humiliating defeat of China during the war and so escaped blame. Following the defeat, the government established a new modern army and put Yuan in charge of training it. By 1901, five of China's seven divisional commanders and most other senior officers were Yuan's protégés. His was the country's best trained and most effective army, making him one of the most powerful people in the land. Tang could not have had a better patron.

In October 1896, Tang was appointed consul-general of China

in Korea. During his time there, he met his second wife, a Korean. In September 1898, he returned home because of the death of his father, ending nearly 10 years of service in Korea. It had been a rapid education for him in world real-politik; he had seen at first hand how two ancient dynasties – China and Korea – were no match for another Asian country that had started modernizing less than 30 years before.

Faced with the same external threats as China, Japan had made a 180-degree change and sent its students to Europe and North America to learn the science, technology, industry and military skills it needed to become a modern state. That was how it was able to win a devastating land and sea victory over the giant neighbour of which it had been a tributary state for centuries. The lessons for Tang and other Chinese were clear: only if the country made radical reforms could it save itself from further military defeats and the economic losses that would follow.

Back in China, Tang became Yuan's secretary at the headquarters of the newly created army. He was also appointed managing director of Northern Railways. To influence his patron, Tang gave him books about the history of Europe, to show how industrial and technological progress was linked to democracy.

Saved by Herbert Hoover in the Boxer Rebellion

In 1900, Yuan appointed him as head of the Bureau of Foreign Affairs of Shandong province. In the spring of that year, the Boxer Rebellion spread from Shandong to other parts of north and northeast China. Well-armed groups burnt Christian churches, killed foreign and Chinese Christians and threatened officials who stood in their way. On June 5, the Boxers cut the railway line between Beijing and Tianjin.

Tang and his family were living in the foreign concession of Tianjin, where they were trapped together with many foreigners and a number of foreign troops. Christians in Tianjin had also fled from the city to the U.S. consulate, which was in the concession; they were, with foreign missionaries, the main target of assassination by the Boxers.

The foreigners included Herbert Hoover, a future president of the U.S.. A mining engineer, Hoover had arrived with his wife in China in March 1899 to work at the Kaiping coal mine; he was 25. He and his family lived in Tianjin, where he met Tang; the two became friends.

In June 1900, the Boxers besieged the Tianjin concession for almost a month. The Hoovers dedicated themselves to the defence of the area; Hoover guided U.S. Marines around the city, using his knowledge of the local terrain. Even his wife had to use a pistol. In their house, they gave refuge to foreign engineers and technicians. Late one night, an artillery shell fired by the Boxers flew through the back window and exploded, blowing up the front door; Hoover and his wife survived. Tang and his family were living in a nearby house.

A few evenings later, a grenade exploded in the Tang house. When Hoover heard the explosion, he rushed over and carried out Tang's wife who was badly wounded. She did not survive her wounds; their fourth daughter was also killed. The Hoovers gave the Tangs refuge in their home and looked after the other children. They included Tang Mei (唐梅, also known as Tang Bao-yue, 唐寶玥) who later married diplomat Wellington Koo (顧維鈞). Koo became ambassador to France, Britain and the U.S. and a founder member of the United Nations; he represented China at the peace talks at Versailles after World War One. In 1919, Tang Mei visited Hoover in Washington and said: "I am the daughter of Tang Shao-yi. We were with you during the siege of Tianjin."

Tang's wife, named Zhang, was a native of Xiangshan. After her death, Tang took her remains back to Tangjiawan for burial.

Having made his first fortune in China, Hoover left the country at the end of 1901. He became the 31st president of the U.S. in November 1928, as the candidate of the Republican Party.

After foreign forces put down the Boxer Rebellion, Tang was in charge of the takeover of Tianjin from the foreign armies which had occupied it, as well as foreign claims for reparation in Zhili (直隸). He also worked as interpreter for Yuan and his assistant in negotiations with foreign envoys and individuals. At the imperial court, Yuan praised him for his work.

Yuan was promoted to the post of Governor-General of Zhili, an enormous province that covered much of northern China, in 1902. But in the year before that he promoted Tang to the post of Mayor or Daotai (道台) of Tianjin and Superintendent of Customs, an important post in the government, in 1901. The Imperial Maritime Customs Service was set up in 1854 by foreign consuls in Shanghai to collect maritime trade taxes. After two decades of operation, it collected about one third of the revenue of the government in Beijing. By 1900, there were 20,000 people working in 40 main customs houses across China and many subsidiary stations. From 1863 until 1908, its Inspector-General was Robert Hart, an Irishman; he was one of the most important foreigners in China during the second half of the 19th century.

Hart set up a bureau which translated into Chinese works of international law, science, world history and current events as well as a postal service and a central statistical office. There was a large number of foreign staff, mainly British but also German, American, French and later Japanese. It was the only institution of the Chinese government that operated continuously as a single entity between 1854 and 1949.

Because of its key role in raising revenue for the government, the position of superintendent held by Tang was an important one. "I felt that it was a priority to take back management of customs," he said. "This is the Chinese customs. We should use foreigners to work for Chinese. Although this is extremely difficult, I will do my best to achieve this."

In 1903 and 1904, Tang also served as supervisor of Beiyang University (北洋大學) in Tianjin. It had been founded less than 10 years before, modelled on famous European and American institutions of higher learning. He sent 34 of its students to study abroad. In 1905, he encouraged the embassy in Paris to send the first Chinese to the top French military school at St. Cyr; his name was Tang Bao-chao (唐寶潮). In 1951, Beiyang University was re-named Tianjin University.

Fight over Tibet

In 1905-06, Tang completed the greatest diplomatic success of his career – negotiating an agreement with Britain under which it recognized Chinese sovereignty over Tibet. He achieved this despite the fact that, as in all his negotiations with foreign powers, it was they who held the military and economic cards; Tang was always playing with a weak hand. But he was able to use his knowledge of domestic politics in London to end the ambitions of British officials and soldiers in India who had designs on Tibet.

It was in December 1903 that the British Indian Army, under the command of Colonel Francis Younghusband, invaded Tibet. It was the first time the colonial power of India had sent soldiers into this remote region, despite the fact that it represented no threat at all. The stated reason for the invasion was to prevent the region falling under Tsarist Russian influence. Russia had no such plan – the invasion was colonial adventurism. It was a brief and bloody campaign, in which the Tibetans were hopelessly out-gunned by the firepower of the British army. It occupied Lhasa in August

1904 – and found no trace of a Russian presence.

Younghusband signed the *Anglo-Tibetan Agreement of 1904* with the Tibetan local government, with the aim of separating it from China. It allowed the British to trade in three towns in Tibet and called for Tibet to pay an indemnity of 500,000 pounds. It formally recognized the Sikkim-Tibet border and declared that Tibet would not have relations with any other foreign power. The Qing government in Beijing refused to recognize the agreement.

In 1905, the government appointed Tang as plenipotentiary to negotiate with the British in India over the status of Tibet and sent him to Calcutta, then capital of British India. Tang impressed his British counterpart by talking in fluent English about the laws and constitutions of several countries and different aspects of the British Empire. The British side demanded that Tang sign the agreement. He refused, saying that Tibet was not a sovereign country and that he would end the negotiations and return to Beijing. He knew that the invasion, which had been initiated by Lord Curzon, the British governor of India, did not have the support of the government in London.

He returned to Beijing. In 1906, Britain sent an envoy to Beijing, where the negotiations resumed. This time Tang did not speak about laws and constitutions but concentrated on the sovereignty issue. He presented many old maps and documents to prove that Tibet belonged to China. Finally, the two sides signed the *Anglo-Chinese Convention of 1906*, which gave sovereignty back to the Qing government. Britain agreed not to annex Tibetan territory or interfere in the administration of Tibet, while China engaged not to permit any other foreign state to interfere in the territory or in its internal administration.

Tang had correctly analysed the reaction in London. Colonial wars had become increasingly unpopular: public and political opinion was against the waging of a war for no good reason – Russia had no plan to control Tibet. In addition, British people considered a battle on March 31, 1904 at Chumik Shenko as a massacre – 600-700 Tibetans were killed and 168 wounded, against 12 British casualties; the battle pitted Maxim guns and bolt-action rifles against people armed with primitive matchlocks, swords and knives. It was this sentiment in London, among the political parties and the public, which explained why the government was willing to sign the convention. Tang was widely praised in Beijing for his diplomatic skills.

In June 1993, his daughter Tang Bao-shan (唐寶珊) donated to the Zhuhai museum Tang's appointment letter for the talks from the Qing government.

Railways and Manchuria

From 1905-07, Tang was put in charge of foreign loans to develop China's mines and railways. In 1906, he was appointed head of the national railway company and in March 1907, he signed an agreement with the British to build a railway between Guangzhou and Kowloon. The section in British-controlled Hong Kong opened in October 1910 and the extension to Guangzhou a year later; the railway is still running more than a century later, carrying thousands of passengers every day.

The government's aim in appointing Tang was to try to reclaim control of its railway network. Its defeat in the Sino-Japanese war had made it realize the importance of such a network to build a strong military and industrial nation. But it was so weak, financially as well as technically, that it could only rely on foreign countries to finance and operate the lines. The imperial capital, Beijing, was the centre of the network; several lines left from there. Other lines were built in Shandong, Guangdong, from Shanghai to Nanjing and from Kunming to Haiphong in the north of Vietnam. From the 1890s to 1905, nearly all the railways were planned, financed, built and operated by foreign powers, using concessions provided by the government. To encourage development of Chinese-owned lines, the government in 1904 allowed provinces to set up their own railway companies and raise funds by selling shares to the public.

In the three northeast provinces known as Manchuria, the building of railways was essential for economic development. It was a huge area, sparsely populated and with winter temperatures that fell 30 degrees below zero. In 1902, the Russians completed the Chinese Eastern Railway, which connected with the trans-Siberian railway near Chita through Hailar and Harbin in Manchuria to the port of Vladivostok on the Pacific Ocean. It drastically reduced the travel distance and time compared to the main route, which lay completely outside China. In 1898, the Russians also built a 550-mile spur from Harbin to Lushun in the ice-free port of Dalian, in Liaoning province. After losing the Russo-Japanese war of 1904-05, the Russians gave up control of most of this line; the route between Changchun and Dalian became the South Manchuria Railway Company (SMRC) of Japan. This company became the principal instrument of Japan's economic colonization of northeast China.

Fearful of the increasing power of Japan in Manchuria and its control of the railway system, the government appointed Tang the governor of Fengtian (Liaoning) province in April 1907, with the mission of building a Chinese railway network in Manchuria to compete with the SMRC. He negotiated with William Straight, U.S. consul in Shenyang, on how to build such a railway and to establish a new bank in Manchuria. He also asked British companies to invest in a Chinese railway. But he failed. Japan out-flanked him by putting pressure on the investors and negotiating with them.

Loses post

In 1908, Empress Dowager Cixi Taihou died and one of her favourites, Yuan Shi-kai, was forced to retire. Without the backing of this powerful patron, Tang lost his post as Governor of Fengtian (Liaoning).

In October that year Tang went to the U.S. to express the thanks of the government for returning a part of the Boxer Indemnity, to be used to educate Chinese students in the U.S.. He had been one of those to persuade the Qing government to accept the money and use it in education. He set out from Shanghai, going first to Japan and then the U.S. before going on to Europe, returning to Beijing in July 1909.

In 1910, he was named Minister of the Department of Posts but resigned the post soon after.

Key role in end of dynasty

Tang played a key role in the fall of the Qing dynasty in 1911 that followed the successful military uprising in Wuhan on October 10. It was one of the most important moments in China's history – the end of an imperial system that had ruled the country for more than two millennia. The Xinhai revolution was different to those in Britain, France, Russia and other countries: it did not cause a bloody civil war and the execution of the royal family. What is more, Emperor Pu Yi and his family were allowed to live in the Imperial Palace for a further 10 years.

By 1911, the emperor and his court had lost almost all their power. They had passed it to Yuan Shi-kai, vesting him with full military and political power to negotiate on their behalf. So, after the Wuhan uprising, it fell to Yuan to represent the government in negotiations with the revolutionaries. It was a perilous moment: there was suddenly a power vacuum in the world's most populous country. No-one could predict the outcome; revolution and civil war were possible. Yuan designated Tang to negotiate on his behalf. Tang was his confidant and close adviser; the two had worked together for 30 years and Tang was the obvious choice. In early December, Tang and his party left Beijing by train for Wuhan. They arrived on December 11; the revolutionaries insisted that the talks be held in Shanghai, a neutral site that was not controlled by either party. They decided on a venue on Nanjing Road, in the International Concession; the talks began on December 18.

The lead negotiator for the revolutionaries was Wu Ting-fang (伍廷芳). He was even more untypical of an average Chinese than Tang. Born in 1842 in Malacca, Wu had studied at the Anglican St. Paul's Church in Hong Kong and law at University College, London and became the first ethnic Chinese barrister in British history. In 1877, he returned to Hong Kong to practice law and became the first ethnic Chinese unofficial member of its Legislative Council. He also served under the Qing dynasty as minister to the U.S., Spain and Peru from 1896 to 1902 and from 1907 to 1909.

The two men were similar – Cantonese, western-educated, diplomats and more fluent in English than Mandarin; they had known each other before and were sympathetic to the other. Both had spent years in the western world and were favourable to its ideas. During the talks, they probably spoke more English and Cantonese than Mandarin.

The talks went smoothly because the two men shared a similar objective – the establishment of a republic and a democratic government. Wu had initially favoured a constitutional monarchy, like Britain and Japan, but had decided that it would not work in the context of China. So he said that a republic was not negotiable; Tang agreed with him. The two men discussed the form which this would take; they agreed on the formation of a National Assembly. Tang sent the proposal to Yuan in

Beijing, warning that, if he did not agree to it, there would be war. Yuan gave his consent. But a powerful faction within the Qing court strongly opposed this; it demanded that Yuan cancel the agreement and recall Tang. Yuan vacillated. On the one hand, he wanted to modernize the country and make it able to stand up to Japan and the western powers. On the other hand, he was extremely ambitious and wanted the top position in the new order – what if a democratic assembly did not choose him? Initially, at least, he supported Tang.

To show his loyalty to the revolutionaries, Tang joined their party, the Tong Meng Hui (同盟會) which later became the Kuomintang, and supported the appointment of their candidate, Sun Yat-sen, as president. Sun took office in Nanjing on January 1, 1912, as first president of the Republic of China. He appointed Tang as his Prime Minister. Under a deal brokered between Yuan and the republicans, Emperor Pu Yi abdicated on February 2, 1912. He was to be treated like a foreign monarch; he and his court were allowed to remain in their private apartments in the northern half of the Forbidden City and the Summer Palace and were to be given an annual subsidy of four million taels of silver – what a different outcome to the fate of Tsar Nicholas II of Russia and Louis XVI of France.

But the gap between Tang and his patron widened. Yuan came to believe that Tang had made agreements without his approval and that he had been deceived. The new order did not guarantee the top post for himself; he did not accept the idea of Sun becoming president. After the fall of the dynasty, there were two centres of power in China – one based on Yuan who controlled the most powerful army and the other based on Sun, Tang and the revolutionaries. The foreign powers took a wait-and-see attitude; they wanted to preserve their privileges and economic interests in China and would support whoever would protect those interests.

Tang organized his new cabinet. Of the 12 members, nine had studied abroad, including Education Minister Cai Yuan-pei (蔡元培) who had studied in Germany, Navy Minister Liu Guan-xiong (劉冠雄) who had studied in Britain, and Agriculture Minister Song Jiao-ren (宋教仁) who had studied in Japan. Several were members of the revolutionary party.

Tang wanted a complete change. During the talks in Shanghai, he met Sun Yat-sen; the two men shared many of the same ideals and talked in the same Xiangshan dialect of Cantonese.

He brought the cabinet together in Nanjing on March 25 and moved it to Beijing in April. His idea was to combine the idealism of Dr. Sun and the military and political strength of Yuan. But he could not realize his ambition. Yuan remained a totalitarian ruler who wanted to control everything. He did not like Tang choosing his own people for the cabinet. He demanded that Tang agree to a request by foreign banks to investigate the new government's finances; Tang refused. Then Yuan rejected his choice of Wang Zhi-xiang (王芝祥), a member of the revolutionary party, as governor of Zhili, even after its provincial assembly had voted for him. Yuan chose his own candidate.

In the battle between these two forces, Yuan controlled most of the aces; he had the army and money. Sun and Tang had neither. Sun resigned on March 10, 1912 after less than three months in office, to be succeeded by Yuan. Tang resigned on June 15, saying that Yuan had deceived the people and sacrificed national interest for his own personal benefit. The two men had worked closely for 30 years; but Tang could not accept Yuan's ambition to be the supreme ruler and reverse the changes of the revolution.

Disgusted by politics

Deeply disappointed by what he had seen in Beijing, Tang moved to Shanghai, the city ruled by the foreign powers. He became chairman of the board of Golden Star Life Insurance Company (金星人壽保險公司).

In March 1913, at a Shanghai railway station, a gunman shot dead Song Jiao-ren; most people, including Tang, believed that Yuan had ordered the assassination. Tang was enraged. He was invited to join future governments but refused.

His home in Shanghai was a large mansion at number 40 Ferguson Road (now Wukang Lu) in the French Concession. In a report of it published by an American newspaper of September 18, 1916, the Associated Press described a large European house surrounded by a wall and a big garden bright with tropical flowers and foliage. The house had many verandas and reception rooms, which were full of Chinese waiting to meet Tang. A wealthy man, he loved antique furniture and porcelain, which he collected during his visits abroad and across China.

In December 1915, Yuan declared himself emperor. Tang and Cai Yuan-pei sent him a telegram, telling him to resign and give up his ambition to be emperor. His reign lasted less than three months, one of the shortest in Chinese history; he died of uremia on June 5, 1916, at the age of 56. After his death, Tang felt more optimistic about China's future, under the leadership of Dr. Sun. The new Prime Minister, Duan Qi-rui (段祺瑞), set up a cabinet and appointed Tang as Foreign Minister. On September 17, Tang went to Beijing to take up the post; but the warlords opposed him and he resigned on September 29. In August the next year, Dr. Sun appointed him as Finance Minister but he could not take up the post because of infighting among the different factions.

In 1919, he sent a telegram to the government saying that he supported the May 4 movement. This had been organized by students from 13 universities in Beijing to protest the terms offered to China by the victorious Allies at the Versailles Peace Conference; they awarded the German concessions in the eastern province of Shandong to Japan, instead of returning them to China. The students protested against the weakness of their government and its inability to protect the national interests at the conference. Students across China followed their example, as well as workers and merchants in Shanghai who launched a general strike.

Tang sent a telegram to Wellington Koo, his son-in-law who was China's representative in Versailles, and asked him not to sign the treaty because he considered it unjust to China. The protests were successful and China did not sign the agreement. It made a separate treaty with Germany. Despite this, Japan was able to gain control of those parts of Shandong and islands in the Pacific which it had obtained during World War One.

Return to Tangjiawan

Tang was increasingly disillusioned with the politics of the central government and unwilling to be involved in them. From 1917-22, he served as an elder statesman in the governments established by the republicans in Guangzhou. In 1920, he moved back to his home township of Tangjiawan. He refused several offers to return to the government, including one to be Foreign Minister in 1924 in the government of Duan Qi-rui. He was a man of conviction and could not tolerate the interference of generals and warlords in politics; his standards were too high for the country into which he was born. In 1928, he was offered land in Nanjing, the new capital, to build a house; many officials were taking advantage of their high position to speculate in land in the city where prices were soaring. But Tang refused.

In 1929, he became chief of his home county of Zhongshan; previously Xiangshan, it was re-named in honour of its most famous son, Sun Zhong-shan (Sun Yat-sen). By then, Tang was a very wealthy man, one of the richest in Guangdong province. "During his life, he made many investments, in mining, railways, insurance and banking," his grandson Tang Jing-tan said. "He had many shares. Two of the four biggest companies in Shanghai – Sincere and Da Xing – were founded by men from Tangjiawan. He had shares in them. He had homes in Shanghai, Tianjin and Beijing. The one in Beijing was close to the Imperial Palace and the one in Tianjin in the foreign concession. Dr. Sun Yat-sen once took refuge there. The family also had homes in Hong Kong and Macao."

Tang wanted to turn Zhongshan into a model county. This was politics on the local level, with which he was more comfortable; he could control what went on in his own county, which he could not do in national ministry. He moved the county seat from Zhongshan to Tangjiawan and a spacious home at Wang Ci Shan Fang (望慈山房) which he had built that year, with a large garden, and named in memory of his mother. It was both his home and the seat of the government.

Tang introduced public buses and built a drainage system that brought running water and toilets into the homes of the township as well as building underground wells that are in use until today. Another of his achievements was the laying of one of the first concrete roads in a rural area of China. Tang developed agriculture and a silver mine. And on top of all that he also set up a commercial port with a customs station that collected revenue for the government from incoming and outgoing cargo; previously, smuggling had been rampant in the area.

The county kept some of the money; the rest went to the central government. Local people called him the "plain-clothes county chief" (布衣縣長) because he often mixed with them. He built roads and hospitals; he operated a clean government and did not tolerate corruption. Many of these projects were funded from his own pocket; the county itself generated little and funds from Nanjing were minimal. Chairman Mao later praised him as one of the rare officials who chose to move from the central government with its perks and privileges to his home county; most officials only want to go the other way. While Tang lived close to his office, he entertained guests at a spacious property nearby, Gong Le Yuan, which he had bought in 1910 and developed into an attractive and well laid-out garden.

But, even in his home county, he could not escape the curse of Chinese politics. He had made an enemy of a Guangdong warlord named Chen Ji-tang (陳濟棠), who was jealous that Tang's fame and popularity exceeded his own. In October 1934, Chen surrounded Tang's home with armed soldiers, on the pretext of asking for soldiers' back pay, and forced him to resign. In 1936, after another confrontation with Chen, Tang left Tangjiawan and moved to his house in the French concession in Shanghai. He had had enough. After he left, he donated Gong Le Yuan to a village committee, a non-government organization, because he wanted to leave it to his hometown. He retained in his possession other properties in the township.

Japanese invasion

When he moved to Shanghai, Tang was 74; he was entitled to peace and quiet. But he did not find it. In 1937, Japan launched their all-out war on China. Between August and November, one million soldiers were involved in a devastating battle for Shanghai that involved fighting from street to street and house to house. Finally, through superior equipment and firepower, the Japanese army captured the city, after losing 93,000 of its soldiers killed, injured or missing; Chinese casualties were 333,500. It was one of the largest battles of World War Two. The fighting was concentrated in areas of the city under Chinese control and not the foreign concessions where Tang lived. Japan was not yet able to attack the western powers at the same time as it attacked China. In December, the Japanese forces went on to capture Nanjing, the national capital, and the government of Chiang Kai-shek (蔣介石) moved to Chongqing deep in the interior.

After taking over large areas of China, Japan wanted to set up a government to rival that of Chiang and help it administer the occupied territories. The Nationalist party was split. A majority believed in continuing the war, in the hope that the western powers would join China. A minority believed that China could not defeat Japan and that the western colonial powers were a greater threat; they favoured collaboration with Tokyo and limiting the loss to life and property that would be caused by continuing the war. Each wanted Tang on their side; he was a former Prime Minister who had been a senior member of the Nationalist Party for more than 20 years. His presence would bring prestige and support to whichever side he joined.

Before the Japanese attack, Tang had sent his family from Shanghai to the safety of Hong Kong. The government in Chongqing sent agents to his house, asking him to leave Shanghai and join them. For their part, Japanese representatives and their Chinese collaborators tried to persuade him to join a pro-Japanese government. On January 19, 1938, the *New York Post* quoted unnamed sources as saying that, despite having retired from national politics for more than 15 years, Tang would lead a national cabinet in Nanjing supported by Japan. It said that he was an enthusiastic collector of jade and porcelain and a keen poker player. Among those who met Tang was Kenji Doihara (土肥原賢二), head of the Japanese secret service in China and a fluent Mandarin speaker. He invited him to head a pro-Japanese government.

On the morning of September 28, 1938, a Chinese group sympathetic to Japan met Tang at his home. Two days later, a man visited the house and stabbed him to death. There are different versions of what happened. According to one, the assassin was Zhao Li-jun (趙理君), a graduate of the Huangpu military academy and one of most trusted agents of Dai Li (戴笠), the spy master of Chiang Kai-shek : Dai's official title was Director of the Investigation and Statistics Bureau. Tang had a bodyguard at the door of his reception room. Zhao entered the room with the excuse of discussing a purchase of porcelain, one of Tang's favourite items; he used a knife concealed in his trouser pocket to stab Tang and shut the door on the way out. He told the bodyguard: "He is waiting for me. I am going to choose even better porcelain for him. Please wait for me, I will be right back." He went to a car waiting for him outside. When staff later found the body, they rushed Tang to hospital. But he had lost a lot of blood; it was too late. Zhao's motive was to prevent Tang joining a pro-Japanese government.

The following is the account of his grandson Tang Jing-tan: "Tang had stayed in Shanghai to clear up certain matters. He planned to go to the U.S., at the invitation of President Roosevelt. He had met Doihara; his fame was greater than that of Wang Jing-wei (汪精衛, the man who later headed the pro-Japanese government). But he told him that he was too old and not interested in taking part in a government. The assassin entered the house with the excuse of showing my grandfather a vase. He had two Russian bodyguards (who stayed out of the room); the assassin asked the bodyguards to fetch something. Inside the vase he had concealed the weapon he used to kill Tang. The decision was taken by the Nationalist spy chief in Shanghai, without the approval of Chiang Kai-shek. Communications then were not as fast as they are today. The Japanese would not have dared to touch Tang, because he was too old and too well-known."

After the war, Doihara was tried for war crimes at the Tokyo International Military Tribunal for the Far East and sentenced to death. He was hanged in Sugamo prison in Tokyo on December 23, 1948.

The murder was a tragic mistake. Tang had no desire or intention to take part in a pro-Japanese government. With his connections and many relatives in the U.S., he had the means and money to emigrate there. But some within the Nationalist party feared that he would collaborate and ordered his assassination.

Chiang Kai-shek and his government believed in him. They set aside 5,000 yuan for his funeral and issued a decree in his honour. They ordered that his life be included in the national history.

His friend Herbert Hoover praised him as a "righteous, capable and ambitious man who had great aspirations for China's future".

Legacy

Tang had a large family. He had three wives, six sons and 13 daughters; of the 19, 13 reached adulthood, including four sons. His first wife died in Tianjin, of the wounds she sustained in the shelling by the Boxers. The second was the Korean he married during his assignment there. According to Tang Jing-tan, she died aged about 30 of a cold; "it was shortly after the birth of my father, Tang Zhu (唐柱) in Tianjin. The Empress Dowager in Beijing summoned her for a meeting, which no-one could refuse. The roads were poor and she fell ill during the journey."

His third wife was Wu Wei-qiao (吳維翹): "Wu Ting-fang introduced her to Tang. She was from a wealthy family in Chengde and a graduate of Dong Hu University (東湖大學). From 1932 to 1938, she lived in the family house in Hong Kong."

His family is scattered across the world, because he sent many of his children abroad to study. One of his daughters married Wellington Koo, whom he selected as a son-in-law when he was in the U.S. in 1908. Koo served as ambassador to the United States, France and Britain and was one of the founding members of the United Nations in 1945.

On January 25, 2013, Tang Shao-yi's 13th daughter, Tang Bao-shan (唐寶珊) died in Australia at the age of 83, the last born of Tang's children and the last to pass away. Born in 1930, she went at the age of five with her parents to Shanghai. She went to the U.K. and studied nursing and then worked in a hospital in Hong Kong. There she met and married Cao Pei-qing, a doctor of western medicine; the two went to settle in Australia. After he died in 2008, she lived with their only son in Sydney. In

June 2012, the two made their last visit together to Zhuhai to honour their ancestors and visit family members. In 2004, she gave 60,000 yuan to the Xiangzhou Education Promotion Association. She also gave HK$60,000 to the Tangjiawan Middle School, to build a library. She gave tens of thousands of yuan for education and cultural preservation in the city and, in recognition of her generosity, was named an honorary citizen.

Tang enjoyed an expensive lifestyle and loved antiques, bronzes and porcelain. He left his spacious home in Shanghai and other cities, including several properties in Tangjiawan.

His greatest legacy is the magnificent park that he bequeathed to his hometown. Now called the Gong Le Yuan, it covers an area of 34,000 square metres (six hectares) and is the most famous tourist attraction in Tangjiawan. It has thousands of trees, including 300 foreign varieties, which Tang brought back with him from his travels. They include trees from Korea, India, Thailand, Malaysia and the Philippines. He bought the property in 1910. He levelled a hill and expanded it in 1914 and 1921, adding a tennis court and a man-made lake with a zig-zag stone causeway, a copy of what he had seen in the West Lake of Hangzhou. He chose the site because of its feng shui, with rolling hills and a view of the sea.

Within the park, he built an elegant three-storey building where he had his office and entertained visitors, including Herbert Hoover, Mei Lan-fang (梅蘭芳), the famous Beijing opera performer, and Wang Jing-wei, the number two in the Nationalist Party who went on to lead the government that collaborated with Japan. On the tennis court, he played the game with his guests.

The garden has rare trees, some of them over 100 years old, including the eucalyptus citriodora planted by Mei Lan-fang and podocarpus macrophyllus planted by Tang himself.

One building has been turned into a museum, with evocative pictures of an extraordinary career: the young Tang in a group of Chinese students in the U.S., stiff and uneasy in their strange setting: a photo with a British general after the negotiations over Tibet: the first cabinet of the Republic of China, so full of hope and optimism: his letter to his son-in-law asking him to reject the Treaty of Versailles; and a letter in 1938 - in English - from a senior Nationalist official asking him to approach the Japanese about a possible peace agreement. There is a photograph of the family of Theodore Roosevelt, U.S. president from 1901 to 1909.

One room is full of pictures of him with his four wives and many children, the face getting older and sadder as he sees the young republic destroyed by warlords, political infighting and the Japanese invasion. Unfortunately, many valuable historical letters, documents, diaries, pictures and other items have been lost during the chaos and political campaigns of the last 70 years.

Staff at the park said government officials from all over the mainland came to stand in the middle of a sun roof Tang built on top of his office. It is similar to, but smaller than, the one in the Temple of Heaven in Beijing, with excellent feng shui.

"Mr Tang left them a slogan to repeat," said one of the staff. "It is shengguan facai (升官發財, rise in the bureaucracy and make your fortune). They stand here and pray for good fortune." But Tang designed the staircase that led to the roof in the shape of a coffin (棺材, guan cai), a pun on the slogan.

In 1989, Tang's third wife, Wu Wei-qiao, donated Wang Ci Shan Fang, where he had lived when he was county chief, to the government. It has been converted into an activity centre for old people and has had a brick extension added. In the large garden behind, the township has built a middle school.

Tang Shao-yi (left) after his appointment by Sun Yat-sen (right) as the first Prime Minister of the Republic of China.

The first cabinet of the Republic of China, with Tang Shao-yi seated on the right.

The office of Tang Shao-yi in his private estate, Gong Le Yuan (the Park of Public Happiness), in Tangjiawan.

Chapter Six

唐國安
1858 - 1913

Great Educator
Tang Guo-an

Introduction

The son of a modest family, Tang Guo-an was among the second group of students to go to the United States under the programme of Yung Wing. He was in his first year of law at Yale University when the Qing government ordered him home, along with his fellow students. After his return, he had a distinguished career as a teacher, journalist, diplomat, campaigner against opium and university president.

In February 1909, he became a national celebrity with an impassioned speech in English at the first international opium conference, in Shanghai. China was the greatest victim of this global curse, with 85 per cent of global production and as the largest importer. The Chinese and foreign media gave wide coverage to Tang's speech; the conference laid the groundwork for an international drug control treaty signed in The Hague in 1912. He used his eloquence and moral force against the powerful interests that reaped millions of dollars in profits from the trade.

His greatest contribution to China was education. With two associates, he revived the programme of Yung Wing to send Chinese students to the United States, after a lapse of 32 years. They used a portion of money from the Boxer Indemnity which the U.S. chose to give back to China. The Indemnity was the equivalent of about US$330 million which China agreed to pay six foreign countries for damage caused by the Boxer Rebellion of 1898-1900. Like Yung before him, Tang accompanied the first group of 47 students, in September 1909, and oversaw their placement in schools and universities.

Then he established Tsinghua (Qinghua) University (清華大學) as a school to prepare Chinese for study in the U.S.. He persuaded the government to give him an imperial garden of 30 hectares in northwest Beijing as the site for the new university and later enlarged it to 80 hectares. After the Xinhai Revolution of October 1911, the university had to close because a warlord stole its income. Tang was one of the few people left on the campus. He nursed it back to life, winning back the revenue, recruiting high-quality faculty from China and the U.S. and becoming its first president in October 1912. He built one of the most modern universities in the country; its graduates were able to move seamlessly into U.S. colleges and achieve excellent academic results. He laid the foundations for what has been one of the top two universities in China; over the past 100 years.

Unfortunately, the strain of building Tsinghua devastated his health; in the spring of 1913, he discovered that he had heart disease. On August 21, he sent a letter of resignation to the Foreign Ministry, asking for his deputy to replace him. The very next day, he died of heart failure, at the age of 54. A large number of mourners, both Chinese and foreign, attended the memorial which the university organized for him; it was a measure of the high esteem in which he was held by both communities.

He was a man of deep conviction, arising from his Confucian upbringing and strong Christian faith.

Early life

Tang was born into a modest family on October 27, 1858 in Jishan (鷄山村) village, Tangjiawan. His father was Tang Tao-fu (唐陶福). The family home was a two-room, one-storey grey-brick house which still stands in Jishan, next to a museum in his memory and a secondary school named after him. He began his studies at a traditional private school in Tangjiawan.

Thanks to Tang Ting-shu, his clan uncle, he was recommended as one of the 120 students to go to the U.S. by the government, under the scheme organized by Yung Wing. In 1872, he went to study for a year at the preparatory school Tong Wen Guan (同文館) which Yung had established in Shanghai; the most important subject was English.

He left in 1873, one of the second group of 40; Tang Shao-yi, another native of Tangjiawan, was in the same group. He went first to Springfield, Massachusetts, where he lived in the house of a Miss D.T. Hall; he studied for two years at a local school, to prepare him for secondary school. Then he moved to Northampton High School in Northampton, Massachusetts and in June 1879 graduated top of his class of 17, together with another Chinese, Liang Poo Chong. Then he went to Phillips Exeter Academy in Exeter, New Hampshire; founded in 1781 with a strong religious background, this was one of the most exclusive private schools in the U.S.. Many of its students, then as now, go on to the top universities in the country. Before Tang's arrival, an American president (Franklin Pierce) and the sons of two others (Ulysses Grant Jr. and Robert Lincoln) had studied there. Robert, the son of Abraham Lincoln, went on to become the Secretary of War.

In Exeter, he lived in the home of Laura Graves. His American hosts took him with them to church on Sundays and he decided to be baptized; his Christian faith would become one of the most powerful influences of his life.

Pictures in his memorial museum in Jishan village show the spacious houses in which the students lived; only wealthy and upper-middle class Americans lived in such comfortable homes. The students had joined the elite of U.S. society.

After graduation from Phillips Exeter, he was admitted into the law department of Yale University. He joined the Delta Kappa Epsilon fraternity. During his studies, he saved money which he sent to his mother in distant Tangjiawan.

He spent one year in Yale and won a second grade prize for Latin, after taking an exam in which 200 students took part. But, unfortunately, he was unable to complete his studies, because the Qing government ordered all the students to return home. Tang went back to China during his second year in the law faculty. He was proud of his time at Yale and maintained contacts with its alumni throughout his life.

The *New York Times* described the Chinese as "keen to study, intelligent and wise, able to overcome many difficulties in studying and achieving standards our own American students would find it hard to achieve". Tang was a typical example. Mindful of the precious opportunity he was being given, he was diligent and focused, overcoming the language barrier to become an excellent student in the fierce competition at two of the U.S.'s elite academies. This education and Christian atmosphere at the schools and the families who hosted him gave him a strong religious faith and sense of morality. These served as an important compass for the rest of his life, during which he would face war, revolution, corruption and the inequality of Chinese and foreigners. He maintained a close connection with the Christian church and its institutions for the rest of his life.

The students returned home in August 1881 to a cold welcome in Shanghai. A total of 96 returned, out of the 120 sent to the U.S.; the others had died, had come back early or chose to stay on. Twenty-one were given work at once; but those in the second and third group, including Tang Guo-an, were detained in a college in Shanghai (求志書院), so that they could undergo re-training as "Chinese". Many in the government considered them unreliable because they had stayed away too long and been Americanized; some called them "fake foreign devils" (假洋鬼子). The government banned them from working for foreign governments and companies – the very institutions most likely to hire them, because of their language skills and experience abroad. With reason, the government said it had paid the substantial costs of study and living for them to study in the U.S.; therefore, they must work for the government on their return, to pay back this investment.

Return to China

After several months of this "re-education" in Shanghai, Tang was sent to a hospital in Tianjin run by a missionary doctor named John Kenneth Mackenzie, to study medicine. Like the other students, he was not consulted about whether he wished to go – it was government officials who decided.

Tang found that he was not interested in medicine; so he made the excuse that his mother was ill and left.

In 1883, he went to work for British trading company, Jardine Matheson. The next year he married Kwan (關) Yueh-kwai, the daughter of Kwan Yung-fa, a wealthy Hong Kong businessman.

From 1884-87, he worked as a translator at the U.S. consulates in Tianjin and Zhanjiang in Guangdong and at an American trading company Russell & Co. (旗昌洋行).

All these jobs were illegal since the government banned him from working for foreigners. Unfortunately, someone reported him and he faced severe punishment. But thanks to the intercession of Patrick Williams, the U.S. consul in Tianjin, he was able to escape with a fine of 2,000 taels of silver, which went toward the tuition fees he owed at the hospital in Tianjin and the years of study in the U.S.. The money was provided by his uncle Tang Ting-shu, who had been his guarantor in the U.S.. From now on, he would have to work for the government, in ministries or state companies.

From 1890-99, Tang Guo-an worked in the Kaiping Mining and Engineering Company established by his uncle, where he was assistant and English secretary to the president of the company. From 1899-1900, he was appointed master of Yingkou (營口) station on the government-owned railway line between Beijing and Shenyang.

Then he became a teacher at St. John's College in Shanghai. This was an Anglican institution founded in 1879 on the banks of the Suzhou Creek; it taught mainly in Chinese. In 1891, it switched to teaching in English. In 1905, it became St. John's University and was registered in Washington D.C., giving it the status of a domestic university in the U.S.. As a result, its students could go directly to graduate schools there. From 1907, it was the first institution in China to grant bachelor's degrees. Over the next 40 years, it attracted some of the brightest and most talented Chinese; they left their marks in many fields, at home and overseas. Tang was active in student affairs and the Young Men's Christian Association at the college.

During the Boxer Rebellion from 1898-1901, Tang was a target; the Boxers chose to assassinate missionaries – "foreign devils" – and Chinese Christians – "secondary devils" (二洋鬼子). He had to flee to the safety of Hong Kong, where he founded the Young Men's Christian Association and served as its first board chairman.

After foreign troops had put down the rebellion, Tang returned to Shanghai in 1903 and became chief accountant for the Canton-Hankow railway (粵漢鐵路). Work on the route, 1,096 kilometres long, began in 1898 and was not completed until 1936. Tang worked for the railway company for four years. He also took a leadership role in the Shanghai YMCA, becoming a committee member and treasurer, setting up a newspaper for the members and helping found braches in Beijing. He was also involved in other voluntary organizations.

At the end of 1903, he set up the Yale Alumni Association. For Tang and many of those like him who had returned from the U.S., Shanghai was the best city in China to live in. With most of the city controlled by foreign powers, it offered a space and liberty not available in other Chinese cities. They could speak, write and organize in a way that would not have been allowed elsewhere. It is no coincidence that the

Communist Party was established in the city's French concession in July 1921, out of reach of the central government and its police.

Tang had a strong sense of personal and social morality: he regarded it as his mission to improve the moral standards of his native country. There was so much to do. A century and half of decay of the Qing Dynasty had led to many phenomena repugnant to Tang and those like him – foot-binding of women, widespread opium-smoking, corruption of government and the business world, low standards of public hygiene and inequality between Chinese and foreigners. He began to speak and write on these themes, campaigning against foot-binding and the opium trade. His reputation grew gradually.

Founded newspaper

It was with this mission that, in Shanghai on August 23 1905, he, Yan Hui-qing (馬惠慶) and other associates founded the country's first bilingual English-Chinese newspaper *Nanfang Bao* (南方報) (*Southern Daily*), mainly aimed at the foreign residents of the city; it aimed to express the viewpoint of Chinese. Published six days a week, it carried news about China and campaigned for better public morality, an end to corruption and "the suppression of evil and the spreading of goodness".

Each week it carried a commentary, many written by Tang and Yan. They were forthright, addressing controversial subjects and not afraid to attack those in power. They criticized the foreign-controlled Municipal Council, which governed the foreign concession, for its policies toward the Chinese residents of the city. Like Yung Wing and others who had studied in the U.S., Tang could not accept the status of being a second-class citizen in his own country.

At Yale, he had been well treated by faculty and fellow students and was not subject to discrimination on grounds of race. But, at home, he found himself looked down upon by foreigners. They enjoyed immunity from Chinese law; if they beat him up or even killed him, they could not be arrested by Chinese police nor tried by a Chinese court. They could be dealt with by police and judges from their own country only. To make matters worse, Tang was more educated and sophisticated than many of the foreigners with whom he came in contact – but was their legal inferior.

This campaigning did not endear Tang and his colleagues to the Municipal Council, who wanted to shut down the newspaper. It did not survive long, closing in 1906. It re-opened under new management in August that year and, at the end of 1907, became a Chinese paper. It closed in February 1908 after two and a half years.

Diplomatic life

His work as a journalist, campaigner and teacher brought Tang to the attention of the Foreign Office in Beijing. It was urgently in need of people with foreign-language skills and the experience of dealing with the western countries who were increasingly involved in China. Tang had just such a profile; since his return to China in 1881, he had been involved in public life and had many friends and contacts among the foreign community. The Foreign Office wanted to recover the sovereign rights which China had ceded to the western powers and Japan through the unequal treaties. Along with other returnees from the U.S., Tang was committed to this task. He joined the Foreign Ministry in 1907.

The ministry gave him his first assignment on the Beijing-Shenyang railway. This line was built by the government to serve Beijing and the main city in the northeast region of Manchuria. Tsarist Russia and Japan were active in building railway lines in the region; the government wanted to ensure Chinese interests were represented and that this strategic sector was not completely under foreign control.

Tang also served as English interpreter and secretary for high officials of the government, including Yuan Shi-kai, who was at that time Viceroy of Zhili province and a cabinet minister. Zhili was one of the most important provinces in China, spreading over what is today Beijing, Tianjin and the provinces of Hebei, Western Liaoning, Northern Henan and the Inner Mongolia Autonomous Region. At the end of 1907, Tang accompanied the Special Commissioner for Investigations (資政院) on a visit to Japan.

In 1908, Tang went with senior civil and military officials to Xiamen to meet the commanders of the U.S. Pacific Fleet. While he was there, he met a delegation of Filipino Chinese who explained their difficulties in entering the Philippines after returning to China to meet their family; the Philippines was under American control. The next day he and his superiors met the commanders of the Pacific Fleet in Guliangyu, a district of Xiamen, and quickly resolved the issue. The *New York Times* reported the story on June 28, 1908.

Tang then went to work on two major China-U.S. initiatives – ending the international opium trade and resuming the education of Chinese students in the U.S..

Fighting opium

It was Charles Henry Brent, the American Anglican bishop of Philippines since 1901, who wrote to President Theodore Roosevelt about the seriousness of opium abuse in the Philippines and proposed that China and the United States hold an international conference on the issue. The president accepted the idea and, after more than a year of complex negotiations among different countries, they agreed to hold the event from

February 2 to 26, 1909 in Shanghai.

This narcotic was a global scourge of which the worst victim was China. In 1906/7, global production was estimated at 41,600 metric tons, almost five times more than illicit opium production in the world a century later. China produced 85 per cent of this total, India 12 per cent and Persia 1.5 per cent. Opium production in Afghanistan, today the world's leading producer, was very modest at that time.

The largest exporter at that time was India, followed by Hong Kong and Singapore, which were mainly re-exporters, not producers. The largest global importer was China, with 3,300 tons; the largest European importer was Britain with 386 tons, most of it re-exported. Opium was the most disastrous consequence of China's interaction with the western powers since the first half of the 19th century, in human, financial and moral terms.

After its defeat in the Second Opium War in 1860, it had been forced to legalize opium; substantial domestic production and imports began. By 1906, 27 per cent of China's adult male population regularly used opium – 13.5 million people consuming 39,000 tones a year. It was a disaster for the smokers and their families and for the country commercially. Prior to the first Opium War in 1839, China had a surplus in its trade with Britain, enabling it to increase its reserves of silver. The increasing import of opium turned this surplus into a growing deficit. In Britain, meanwhile, the *Pharmacy Act of 1868* restricted the sale of opium to professional pharmacists; the Society for the Suppression of the Opium Trade was set up in London in 1874. While the British government worked hard to protect its people from opium, it was happy for Chinese to smoke it.

International companies in China benefited greatly from the trade; many foreigners regarded opium-smoking as a sign of the moral decay of the Chinese race. They laid blame not on the suppliers but on the consumers, saying that it was their choice to spend money on opium and a sign of a weak and incompetent government that could not control such practices. But one group of foreigners was implacably opposed – the missionaries.

At the 1890 Shanghai missionary conference, they organized the Anti-Opium League in China, with branches in every mission station; an American missionary named Hampden Coit Du Boise was its first president. It published books and pamphlets and campaigned against the drug, in China and abroad. Tang was close to these missionaries, shared their convictions and was active in campaigning against opium in Shanghai. They believed the campaign at home needed foreign support. Chinese established anti-opium societies, which worked to turn public sentiment against the drug, by holding mass meetings at which opium tools were burnt and speakers explained the terrible consequences of addiction. In 1906, the government issued regulations outlawing the drug, but with limited effect.

Thanks to these efforts by Chinese and foreigners the first international conference on the subject was held in Shanghai in February 1909, entitled the International Opium Commission. It was a commission rather than a conference, a significant difference; the latter would have given delegates the right to draft regulations to which the signatory states would be bound. Instead, it could only make recommendations – a sign of the reluctance of member countries. The original plan was to limit the conference to the situation in Asia; but the issue could only be addressed if the major producing, manufacturing and consuming nations attended. They reached a compromise under which delegates acted in only an advisory capacity to their governments; this allowed most of the colonial powers to attend.

The Chinese delegation was led by the Governor of Guangdong and Guangxi, with Tang one of his three deputies; the government chose Tang to act as spokesman, because of his strong views, his high level of education and his fluent English.

Even before the event, it had an impact. Countries instigated reforms in order to be able to show progress at the meeting. As a result, a number of countries reported significant declines in their opium imports and sales before 1909. The most important of these changes made before the conference was the bilateral agreement which bound Britain to gradually eliminate its opium sales to China and China to eliminate its own poppy cultivation between 1908 and 1917.

The conference opened on February 2, at the Palace Hotel on the Bund; it is now the southern building of the Peace Hotel. A plaque outside the door commemorates the event. There were delegations from 13 countries – China, U.S., U.K., France, Germany, Russia, Japan, Italy, Holland, Portugal, Turkey, Siam and Persia. The conference provided for the first time a detailed overview of the global situation.

Tang delivered his speech in fluent English and answered questions raised by the British and Dutch delegates. While saying it was hard to know the real figures of production and consumption in China he estimated 1906 production in China at 34,800 tonnes. Of its population of 400 million, about 50 million were adult males, of whom 13,455,699 were opium smokers.

Tang estimated the country's annual loss to opium of 856.25 million taels of silver, in terms of deaths, production lost by smokers and arable land under opium that could grow other crops. He said that imports of opium accounted for 7.5 per cent of China's trade. "The economic losses it causes to the world are so enormous. The whole world cannot allow this any more," he said.

"Opium is the most urgent moral and economic issue facing our country. For China, the outcome of this conference is more important than for any other country. To solve this problem, we must rely on ourselves. But, to solve it, international co-operation is also extremely important." He described the efforts that China was making against the drug. "This issue has aroused the anger of the entire nation, from north to south, from east to west, and every class – officials, students, gentry, farmers and the humblest worker. Everyone is united in their determination to rid the country of this scourge. The greatest hope for a final victory depends on making use of this anger."

He also analysed how much the opium trade was damaging the country's progress and modernization; he called on the colonial power to abolish the unequal treaties concerning opium. He also spoke of the moral aspect of the problem, saying that the principles of both Confucianism and Christianity called for a ban. "We must remember that there is a law above the laws of man, above the rules of economics and above the laws of nature and that is the law of the eternal Lord. In the words of Confucius, 'What you would not do to yourself, do not do unto others' and, in the words of Jesus, 'You should love your neighbour as yourself'." The speech moved his audience and the public. It was widely reported by the Chinese media, which described it as clear, logical and persuasive. It was a milestone in China's fight against opium.

The *North China Herald* published the full speech in its edition of February 6; it was widely reported in Britain and the rest of Europe. William Wirt Lockwood, secretary of the Shanghai YMCA, said that the speech was full of wisdom and passion and expressed China's demands to the colonial powers. "He did far more than anyone else in persuading the British government to change its policy of opium trade with China," said Lockwood.

The commission closed with the adoption of nine recommendations, on the prohibition of planting, smoking and trafficking of opium and its derivatives, including action to stop the trade in the foreign concessions within China.

It laid the groundwork for the first international drug control treaty, the *International Opium Convention of The Hague*, which was signed in 1912. It formally established narcotics control as an element of international law.

Tang was one of three representatives of China at the Opium Convention meeting in The Hague, in December 1911 and January 1912. Before the meeting, he travelled to Europe and the U.S. to collect information about it. He also used the time to prepare for the next great mission of his life – the foundation of Tsinghua University.

Education in the U.S.

Like Yung Wing and others who had studied in the U.S., Tang believed strongly in the value of overseas education and that it was the best way to turn China into a strong, modern nation. He was outraged by the refusal of the Qing government to allow Chinese children to study abroad. How could China become a modern state? Every day he saw the results of the policy – foreigners were given important jobs within the government, industry, commerce and education, with generous salaries and conditions, because there were no Chinese qualified to do them. In government and commercial negotiation with foreigners, Chinese were handicapped by their lack of knowledge, skills, technology and foreign languages; the economic loss to individuals, companies and the state was incalculable.

Suddenly, out of the blue, an opportunity came to resume a programme that had been ended abruptly more than 30 years before. It arose from the opposition in the U.S. to accept the full amount of the indemnity to be paid by Beijing as punishment for the Boxer Rebellion. The government had agreed to pay 450 million taels of silver – worth about

US$330 million at the time – with an interest of four per cent a year for 39 years. The U.S. share was 7.32 per cent, more than it had originally demanded.

China's ambassador to Washington, Liang Cheng, started a campaign to persuade the U.S. to return the difference between what it had demanded and what it received; Liang had gone there at the age of 12, as part of the Yung Wing mission, and studied at Phillips Academy and Amherst College. The American ambassador in Beijing proposed that this money be used for education; American missionaries in China also campaigned for this.

In 1907, President Theodore Roosevelt accepted these proposals, believing that using money to fund the education of Chinese in the U.S. would leave them with pro-American sentiments. He decided to set aside US$11 million of the US$24 million his government was due to receive for this purpose. The two countries signed an agreement in October 1908. The money would be used to fund the selection, training and transportation of students to the U.S. and their study there. In the first four years, starting in 1909, 100 would leave each year and 50 a year from the fifth year; the agreement called for the programme to continue until 1940.

In June 1908, the Foreign and Education Ministries in Beijing set up a U.S. study department to oversee the programme; Tang was put in charge of its daily operations. It was the happiest assignment of his life, a project into which he put his heart and soul. This was a rare and happy occasion when his ambitions matched those of the government. Many of his collaborators were those, like Tang Shao-yi, who had studied with him in the U.S..

In an article he wrote during this period, he outlined the importance of the student programme: "Since the Russo-Japanese war of 1904-5, the territory of China had been invaded by other nations ... We must avoid the fate of Finland, Poland and India. China has reached a critical moment in its history. A country that has too weak an army and navy has no voice in the Hague Court or other international meetings."

He wrote that, for many decades, because China was militarily weak, it had been humiliated time and again and seen its interests taken away. She had lost Japan, Burma and Korea as protectorate countries and lost the territories of Hong Kong, the Penghu islands, Taiwan, Okinawa and what had become the Russian Far East. The cities of Gaozhou bay, Kowloon, Qingdao, Weihaiwei and the Liaodong peninsula were in the hands of foreign powers.

"What is more, China has to pay to the colonial powers an enormous Boxer Indemnity in excess of 100 million taels of silver," Tang wrote. "When they go abroad, Chinese are subject to humiliation of every kind, to hatred and prejudice, even violence and torture. Some countries use laws and treaties to prevent the entry of Chinese. In our country, when the westerners have the right to do trade, the government has lost its rightful powers. They enjoy protection from the law, force us to pay import duty, spread the opium trade and set up military bases in their concessions. They control the foreign trade in our ports and take away our postal rights."

"Our students must be loyal to the government and love the country. Of course, they will be angry with the inability of those who govern us – but this attitude is harmful to the country … When they return, they must forget the past, cherish the future, move bravely forward and make the country great.

"Look at the example of Japan, whose children are all willing to devote themselves to the emperor, a loyalty that has been bred for many generations. We want to make China the most advanced, open and strong country."

In August 1909, the department held its first examination, with three examiners of whom Tang was one. The contrast could not have been greater with Yung Wing's efforts in finding people to go; they were flooded with applicants. Of the 630 candidates, 47 were chosen through a competitive exam.

When they went to the U.S. in September that year, Tang accompanied them; it was a 20-day voyage by sea from Shanghai to San Francisco. From there, they took the trans-Pacific railroad to Springfield, Massachusetts. They were the first Chinese to study in the U.S. since 1881. Tang arranged for them to go to different schools and stay with local families, like the first group; he set out rules for their behaviour. When he was satisfied that all the students were in place and comfortable in their new surroundings, he went back to China. In July 1910, his department held a second exam; 70 were chosen as a result.

Tsinghua University

Tang and his colleagues feared that the candidates they chose would not be good enough to study at U.S.. universities. So they proposed establishment of a college in China to prepare them; this is how Tsinghua (Qinghua) university was born. The government accepted the idea and Tang's proposal to use a former imperial park of 30 hectares in northwest Beijing that had fallen into ruin.

The building expenses were covered by the funds from the U.S. government. Work began at the end of 1910, on classrooms, student dormitories and accommodation for faculty, Chinese and foreign. In February 1911, Tang and his staff moved in there and on April 29, it changed its name to Tsinghua College. That was a Sunday and it became the institution's foundation day; there were 460 students and 18 teachers from the U.S.. In June 1911, the third examination was held in the garden of the campus; 63 students were chosen and Tang added a further 12. The exam was strict, so the quality of students was high. They went on to obtain good academic results in the U.S..

In October that year came the Wuhan uprising which sparked the Xinhai Revolution and led to the overthrow of the Qing (covered in more detail in chapter five). The government was in turmoil. Military strongman Yuan Shi-kai appropriated for his army the money set aside for Tsinghua. Suddenly there were no funds; everyone was afraid of what would happen.

In November, Tang ordered an end to the classes. Students and most of the faculty went home; Tang was one of the few people left on the campus. His nephew, Tang Meng-lun, came to his help, providing guns and a 24-man security team to protect the university from attack and damage; they patrolled the campus night and day. Tang went to The Hague to attend the International Opium Convention as one of the three Chinese representatives, in December 1911 and January 1912.

The new government, under President Sun Yat-sen, was established on January 1, 1912. Sun chose as his first Prime Minister, Tang Shao-yi, Tang Guo-an's fellow returnee and friend for many years. Tang Shao-yi looked to the university for talent for his new administration and several professors accepted posts, but Tang declined. He was determined to complete the mission which he had started at Tsinghua.

When he returned from the anti-opium conference in The Hague in early 1912, Tang found that most of the staff had left. This gave him the opportunity to create the institution he wanted, a university like no other in China. It adopted a western educational system and presidential responsibility system, with an emphasis on science and technology. Tang wanted a high moral tone; he chose a faculty who were largely Christian and taught "cultivation of the whole person". He also set up a hospital and hired American doctors, to look after the health of faculty and students.

He ruled that, since it was a preparatory school for the U.S., it had to be based on the American model, including the organization of classes, class materials, teaching methods and style of living. Many of the teachers came from the U.S. and many classes and campus activities used English. The university re-opened on May 1, 1912 after being closed for five months. Tang was chancellor. On October 17 the same year, it officially became known as Tsinghua College and Tang was named its first president.

Tang was working at full stretch. He was in charge of recruiting faculty, raising money and planning construction. Many professors had, like him, studied in the U.S. and knew well the standards expected of a university there. The curriculum he designed was equivalent to the first and second year of a U.S. university, so that its graduates could go directly into the third or fourth year of study at a U.S. university or join masters and Ph.D programmes. There was a division between arts and science, with compulsory and elective subjects and special attention to specialized education.

During a visit in November 1920, British philosopher Bertrand Russell said: "You have moved here a university from the U.S.."

To allow room for expansion and make full use of the money from the Boxer Indemnity, Tang acquired two more imperial gardens, Jin Chun Yuan (近春園) and Shen Chun Yuan (申春園), on adjacent sites and bought additional land, bringing the total area to 80 hectares. The additional space enabled him to construct a science building, sport centre, library and large meeting hall.

His biggest headache was obtaining the money due to the university. The new government was weak and unstable. President Sun Yat-sen resigned on March 12, 1912, after less than three months in office, to be replaced by Yuan Shi-kai who took the indemnity money for himself and his army; he paid no heed to Tang's appeals. So Tsinghua did not receive the funds at the proper time; they always arrived late. By August 1912, Tang had borrowed 200,000 taels from two foreign banks, equivalent to one third of annual spending; he could not pay the university's bills. He looked everywhere, asking foreign banks, the Foreign Ministry and the Ministry of Finance for help.

In a letter in July that year to his superiors at the Foreign Ministry, he stressed that the indemnity money was only for the university and should not be considered part of national revenue that could be used as the government wished. The resolution of this issue would guarantee the university's future, he said.

In early 1913, five students from Tsinghua went to the first Far Eastern Games multi-sport competition in Manila. While not a sportsman himself, Tang enthusiastically supported physical exercise for students and young people. He led the team to Manila; it was the first time a Chinese team had taken part in an international sports event.

This stress and uncertainty took a heavy toll on Tang's health. It's no wonder, as he was setting up the first university of its kind in China from scratch and did not know if he would have the funds to pay for it. He was both college principal and main fund-raiser. When he started the project it was under the Qing; then there was a revolution and he was working for the Republic of China. This was a time of instability and confusion. The government had been completely re-organized and most of the officials had been changed.

In the spring of 1913, he discovered that he had a heart condition. His health deteriorated. He wrote: "During the year, I have given half my life to the school and half to paying back the debt." His deputy Zhou Yi-chun (周詒春) took over some of his duties.

Tang was completely exhausted. On August 21, 1913, he sent a letter of resignation to the Foreign Ministry, asking to be replaced by Zhou Yi-chun; he praised Zhou for having a strong sense of responsibility, great love and a long-term vision. He said that, during the last year, he had not taken a single day off and expended enormous energy on finding money. He had been very anxious about it but had received no help. The next day at four o'clock in the afternoon, before the ministry had the chance to approve his request, he died of heart failure, aged 54. In his will, he left his library to the university and said that, after the death of his wife, all his assets should be given to charity.

The university held a memorial service, attended by many people, including senior officials of the Chinese government, diplomats and other foreigners. Those who could not attend, including representatives of the YMCA, sent wreaths.

Zhou lived up to Tang's expectations and proved to be an excellent president.

The college was renamed National Tsinghua University on August 17, 1928. Tang's photo hangs on the wall of its history gallery.

One friend, D.Y. Lin, wrote a moving tribute: "As president of Tsinghua College, he worked unselfishly and gathered around him a host of admirers. No doubt, it was he who had organized and built up that college to what it is today. It is, indeed, most sad to think that he had to yield untimely to the decree of Fate. China has lost one of her best citizens, Tsinghua its unselfish and energetic president and we a most useful friend."

Legacy

Tang Guo-an left behind the sense of a life cut short, a mission incomplete. The new Republic of China was desperately in need of talented people like him, as it struggled to build a new country on the decay and corruption of the last century of Qing rule. Education was at the heart of the new China. To become a modern state and compete with other nations of the world, the country needed young men and women with professional training, foreign languages and an understanding of the outside world. With his education, convictions and passion for learning, Tang was ideally equipped to provide this education. What a tragedy it was that the enormous stress of establishing Tsinghua University during a time of political chaos and instability was too much for his health.

His college friend Chen He-qin (陳鶴琴) wrote in *My Half-Life* (我的半生): "Tang was a Christian, extremely sincere toward other people. He was very diligent in what he did and considered students as his brothers and faculty as friends. For that, he was loved by the students. How sad that he was university president for a short time, then fell ill and died. We all feel extremely sad, as if we have lost a compassionate mother." To remember him, the university made a copper plaque, and put it in the east wall of the main gate. Unfortunately, due to the tumultuous history of Beijing since then, the plaque has disappeared.

Tsinghua and the U.S. study programme were his greatest legacy. Since its foundation, through the rule of warlords, the Kuomintang and the Communists, it has remained one of the top universities in China and produced many of the nation's leaders. Among the graduates of the Boxer Indemnity programme were Nobel physics prize winner Yang Chen-ning (楊振寧), mathematician Chung Kai-lai (鍾開萊), Qian Xue-sen (錢學森), the father of China's rocket programme, and Hu Shih (胡適), president of Beijing University and one of the leaders of China's new literature movement. They also included future presidents of Tsinghua, Zhejiang and Jinan universities.

Museum to him

Today Tang is remembered at Tsinghua and in his home village of Jishan, now part of the special economic zone of Zhuhai. On March 20, 2011, the city opened a museum in his honour, built at a cost of 15 million yuan. It is next to the modest, two-room house where he grew up. In front is a lawn, with an imposing statue of Tang in the middle. It has three floors. There is an exhibition on the second floor, with photographs, maps and historical items from different periods of his life, including the YMCA in H.K., his newspaper in Shanghai that campaigned against foreign privilege and his speeches at the Anti-Opium Conference. It has exhibits of his childhood, school years and professional life, with letters, speeches and photographs. Next to the museum is a secondary school named after him. Both are spanking new red-brick structures, in a beautiful setting in front of rolling hills. The head of the museum is Ban Yong (班勇), who is secretary-general of the Zhuhai Tsinghua Graduates Association.

Unlike other sons of Xiangshan, Tang did not spend money in his ancestral home. During his study years in the U.S., he sent money to his family. But, after his return, he was very busy and spent little time there. He and his wife had no children of their own; they adopted a son.

The man who collected the items for the museum is Yang Yi (楊毅), secretary-general of the Research Institute for the study of Yung Wing and the Chinese children studying in the U.S.. Said Yang: "Tang made a significant contribution to China in four aspects. One was sending Chinese students abroad and training talent. A second was to promote the country's improvement, by campaigning against opium, superstition, foot-binding, the keeping of concubines and other social injustices. The third was to spread Christianity, not through force, commerce or material benefit but for its own sake, and to make it a local religion. The fourth was his work in the media; he was involved in setting up four newspapers, through which he expressed the Chinese point of view. He never considered settling in the U.S..".

Tang Guo-an (second from right) with his fellow students during their time in the United States.

Tang Guo-an, second from left, with other returnees.

The second group of students going to the U.S. under the programme organised by Tang Guo-an, in Beijing in 1910. He is seated at the front on the right.

A teaching building of Tsinghua College in 1911.

Chapter Seven

蔡廷乾
1861 - 1935
Warrior Statesman
Cai Ting - gan

Introduction

Cai Ting-gan had a remarkable career – naval officer, Presidential advisor, head of the National Tax Bureau, diplomat, briefly Foreign Minister, and scholar.

Like Tang Shao-yi, he played an important role in the negotiations between the Qing Dynasty and those who launched the revolution of October 1911. Also like Tang, he learnt many skills during eight years in the United States as one of the fortunate 120 students.

On his return to China, he made full use of what he had learnt; at the Qing court, he was prized for his English-language ability and knowledge of world affairs. Added to this was his valiant service in the Imperial Navy during the Sino-Japanese war of 1894-95; he was wounded and taken to prison in Osaka.

Again like Tang, he owed his promotion at the court to the patronage of Yuan Shi-kai, one of the most powerful officials of the last 20 years of the Qing. And still like Tang, his loyalty wavered after 1911 because of Yuan's refusal to accept a republican government; Cai and Tang broke with Yuan after he declared that he would become emperor.

Cai later held important posts, especially in the fields of tax and finance, became Minister of Foreign Affairs for four months in 1926, before he retired from public life in May the next year.

During his final years, he was active as a teacher at Tsinghua and Yanjing (燕京) universities in Beijing. He wrote books and translations. One of them, *Chinese Poems in English Rhyme*（唐詩英韻）, with 122 poems from the Tang Dynasty, was one of the earliest translations of Chinese poetry into English by a Chinese; it was published by University of Chicago Press in 1932 and received critical acclaim. Because of his skills with the pen and sword, his friends gave him the nickname "Scholar-General" (儒將).

Early life

Cai was born in Shangshan (上柵村) village, Xiangshan on April 15, 1861, the son of an engineer who had studied machinery in Tianjin. He received his early education at a private school in Tangjiawan township. It was this link that gave him the precious opportunity to study in the U.S.. He was living in Tianjin in 1872 with his parents; through his connections with Tangjiawan, his father proposed him to go to the U.S. and Yung Wing agreed. He went to study at the school which Yung had established in Shanghai to prepare the students for the experience.

In 1873, at the age of 13, he left in the second group of 30 students. On arrival, he went to Hartford, Connecticut and lived with two other Chinese students in the house of the A.S. McClean family; they first went to a language school and then studied at the New Britain Middle School. In 1874, Rebekah McClean, the lady who was looking after them, recommended that the three boys, including Cai, be sent back to China because of their mischievous behaviour. Yung interviewed the three and, impressed by their fluent English and their determination to stay on, decided otherwise. He sent Cai and one of the others, Tang Yuan-zhan (唐元湛), to Lowell, an industrial city in eastern Massachusetts; there they studied not liberal arts but mechanics in a factory. During their final year, the two learnt to manufacture cartridges; Cai later said he learnt to make a Gatling gun there. After graduation, he entered the Lowell machinery factory and improved his knowledge of industrial machines.

He lived in the U.S. for eight years. Like most of his fellow Chinese, he adapted well to the new environment; he thought and acted like most of the young Americans around him. He felt increasingly alienated from the closed, feudal system he had left behind. He was one of the first to cut his pigtail, in defiance of his government. Then, in 1881, together with the other students, he was ordered to return to China.

Firing torpedoes at the Japanese navy

After his return, he was assigned to a school in Tianjin for the study of naval mines. He studied there for four years, learning the operations and theory of mines as well as electrical machinery, mining and prospecting; he worked under British, American and French teachers, further broadening his knowledge of science and technology and the outside world. In 1884, he trained under a British naval officer on working at sea and was assigned to a vessel in Fujian province. In 1885, his unit fought in the Sino-French war; this was a conflict between August 1884 and April 1885 for control of Tonkin, northern Vietnam. There were naval battles in Zhejiang, Fujian and Taiwan.

In 1888, Cai was sent to the Beiyang (Northern Ocean, 北洋) Fleet, the largest and most modern of China's four navies. Based in Weihaiwei on the eastern tip of Shandong province, it guarded the Gulf of Bohai, the provinces of Liaoning, Hebei and Shandong and the Chinese tributary state of Korea. He served on a torpedo boat at the Dagukou (大古口) base. In 1892, after three more years of training, he was made commander of the torpedo ship Fulong (福龍).By 1894, the Beiyang Fleet was the best armed of China's navies; between 1881 and 1889, it had acquired eight armoured cruisers, seven of which had been built in Germany and Britain; it also had two battleships, of 7,430 tons, built at the Vulcan shipyard in Stettin (now Szczecin, Poland), then in Germany. The Fulong was one of eight torpedo boats. In numbers, the Beiyang Fleet alone equalled Japan's entire fleet.

The rivalry between the rising power of Japan and the declining power of China came to a head in Korea, which both countries wished to control. War between the two was officially declared on August 1, 1894. On September 15, the Imperial Japanese Army attacked the city of Pyongyang, which was defended by 15,000 Chinese troops. The Chinese were defeated, losing 2,000 killed and 4,000 wounded.

Two days later, Japanese warships encountered the Beiyang Fleet in the mouth of the Yalu River; it was the largest naval engagement of the war. Cai led his Fulong torpedo boat into battle. He aimed to sink one of the Japanese warships and fired a torpedo but the target was too far away and the torpedo missed. With its superior firepower, the warship fired back. The Fulong soon had fired its three torpedoes and had no option but to withdraw from the battle. The better speed, manoeuvrability and artillery of the Japanese navy won an overwhelming victory; it destroyed eight of the 10 warships of the Beiyang Fleet, gaining total command of the Yellow Sea. On their way back, Cai and his men rescued many sailors whose ships had been sunk and who were floating in the water; they returned in despair to their base in Weihaiwei.

The next phase of the war was a Japanese attack on Weihaiwei, to neutralize the Beiyang Fleet. The city was equipped with 12 land fortifications armed with Krupp and Armstrong cannon as well as two fortified islands in the bay; the entrances to the harbour were closed by booms to prevent attacks from outside, with the 29 remaining ships of the fleet anchored inside. Western military observers considered its defences better than those of Hong Kong; some thought it impregnable. The Chinese commander, Admiral Ding Ru-chang (丁汝昌), asked his superiors in Beijing for permission to attack the Japanese fleet at sea, where he considered he had an advantage. But, fearful of losing more ships as they had done at the Yalu River, Li Hong-zhang ordered him to remain in port.

The Japanese did the obvious thing – they attacked by land and not by sea. On January 18, 1895, units of Japan's Second Army began landing at Rongcheng, east of Weihaiwei; within three days the landing was completed without opposition. The attackers timed the assault on the city to coincide with Chinese New Year, the major festival on the calendar, launching the attack on January 30, despite blizzards and temperatures as low as minus 26 degrees Celsius. The Beiyang Army defended the city for nine hours, before abandoning the fortifications largely intact. They fled on February 1, allowing the Japanese to enter the next day without opposition. From there, the Japanese turned the city's guns on the fleet in the harbour. On February 4 they removed the booms, enabling torpedo boats to enter and attack the ships. An attack on February 7 severely damaged the main Chinese battleship and sank three other vessels. The crews of the remaining torpedo ships, including the Fulong, attempted to escape along the coast to Yantai. The Fulong's boiler pipes were damaged, slowing it down. A Japanese ship overtook and captured it, taking Cai and his men prisoner. He had been wounded.

With defeat for the Chinese certain, the Japanese commander, Admiral Sukeyuki Itoh (伊東祐亨), wrote a letter to Admiral Ding, a personal friend: he said that Ding was a patriot who had been consigned to certain defeat by the policies of his government. He offered Ding political asylum in Japan until the end of the war, after which he could return and rebuild his country on a proper basis. In his reply, Admiral Ding thanked him for his friendship but said that he could not forsake his duties to the state. "The only thing now remaining for me to do is to die." Overcome with grief and shame at his defeat, he committed suicide by taking an overdose of opium in his headquarters; four senior commanders followed his example. Cai was sent to prison in Osaka. On April 17, 1895, China and Japan signed the *Treaty of Shimonoseki*, in which China recognized the total independence of Korea and ceded the Liaodong peninsula, Taiwan and Penghu islands to Japan "in perpetuity".

China's defeat was a milestone in the history of Asia. For two millennia, China had been the dominant power in Asia; now it was Japan, despite a land area and population a fraction of that of China. An intense programme of modernization that had started only 27 years before in 1868 had enabled Japan to build a modern army and navy on western lines. China's defeat was not due to a lack of heroism of Admiral Ding, his commanders (including Cai) nor the sailors under him. It was due to the policies of those above them – military and civil leaders embezzled money, even during the war.

The Beiyang Fleet did not purchase any battleships after 1888 and no ammunition after 1891, with the funds being used to build the Summer Palace in Beijing. For the project, the Empress Dowager Cixi Taihou diverted 30 million taels of silver intended for the Beiyang Fleet. The morale of soldiers was poor due to lack of pay, low status and weak leadership and discipline. Ships were not properly maintained; sentries spent their time gambling and sold gunpowder, replacing it with cocoa. These sharp differences between the Chinese and Japanese military were crystal clear to Cai and his fellow officers.

Cai did not spend long in detention. After intervention on his behalf by Yuan Shi-kai, he was freed after the signing of the *Treaty of Shimonoseki* and returned home in April 1895. He was dismissed from the navy, together with all those who had been taken prisoner; it was the Qing government's way of placing blame for the humiliating defeat. After the death of Li Hongzhang in 1901, Cai's rank was restored, together with that of the other officers who had received the same treatment. Out of the navy, Cai had no job. On the recommendation of Tang Shao-yi, he entered the office of Yuan Shi-kai, then governor of Zhili province.

For the next 26 years, Cai played an important role in national life in Beijing. He was active in many departments of the government – the military, customs, tax and finance and diplomacy. He was an interpreter and advisor to Yuan, the most powerful man in China for next 15 years. Yuan hired him for the same reason that he hired his fellow son of

Tangjiawan, Tang Shao-yi. Cai spoke fluent English and understood well the foreigners who exerted so much influence on China, in banking, business, the military and diplomacy. China was an independent state in name only; it had ceded its sovereignty in many sectors and needed people like Tang and Cai to negotiate with the foreigners who controlled the finance, investment, technology, management expertise and arms it needed.

In September 1907, Cai moved to Beijing where he worked in the office of Yuan Shi-kai, who was concurrently Minister of Military Machinery and Foreign Minister. In October that year, he accompanied the Minister of Commerce on a tour of Philippines, Saigon, Bangkok, Java and Malaya; he served as interpreter and advisor to the minister, who praised him for his work. In July 1907, Yuan sent a letter to the court, praising Cai for his technical and engineering skills, his knowledge of foreign affairs and his loyalty; Yuan recommended that the government make the best use of him.

In 1909, Yuan fell out of favour and was sent to live quietly at his native place in Xiangcheng (項城) in Henan province. As his protégé, Cai also had to retire from public life and live quietly in Beijing; Yuan took this as a sign of loyalty. As a result, when Yuan returned to power in 1911, he promoted Cai to the post of vice-admiral and other positions.

Negotiating the revolution

After the Xinhai Revolution in October 1911, Cai played the role of an intermediary between the government and the revolutionaries, like Tang Shao-yi. Yuan picked the two men for the same reasons – both were Cantonese, like many of the rebels, and knew some of them personally. He sent Cai to Wuhan to negotiate secretly with Li Yuan-hong (黎元洪), one of the rebel leaders, who had served under him as third officer of the Fulong torpedo boat. Like Tang Shao-yi, Cai was sympathetic to the establishment of a republic; but his talks did not result in an agreement and he returned to Beijing.

He reported to Yuan the outcome of the talks and introduced him to George Morrison, an Australian who had been *The Times* reporter in Beijing since February 1897. One of the few foreign correspondents in China, Morrison was well informed on the inside workings of the government and the foreign powers watching its revolution. Cai regarded him as a friend, informant and a useful spokesman to the outside world.

On November 16, *The Times* published a 3,000-word report of Cai's talks: it said that, initially, he had favoured a constitutional monarchy but, after talks with the revolutionaries, had switched to a republic. In December, Cai was sent back to Wuhan for more secret meetings with Li Yuan-hong.

On January 18, 1912 Cai wrote to Morrison to say that they had reached broad understanding with the revolutionary party and that he would brief him in person when they met. But Yuan felt the talks were going against his interests and ordered an end to Cai's secret mission. Over the next months, Cai used Morrison to reveal more details of the unfolding revolution.

On February 12, 1912, Emperor Pu Yi abdicated. On February 14, the Provisional Senate voted for Yuan as president, to replace Dr. Sun Yat-sen. On February 16, Yuan had Cai cut his pigtail, the symbol of loyalty to the Qing; he felt uncomfortable having it done by a barber and wanted to share this historic moment with a friend. The news was reported exclusively by Morrison in the newspaper in London the next day.

Cai's status rose even further: he became interpreter and secretary of President Yuan and his liaison officer with Morrison. On August 2 that year, Morrison resigned his position on The Times to become Yuan's political advisor, with the substantial salary of 4,000 pounds a year. Morrison was sent to London to help float a Chinese government loan of 10 million pounds. He later joined the Chinese delegation at the negotiations for a peace treaty in Versailles in 1919 after World War One.

Cai went on to hold more important posts. In December 1912, Yuan appointed him Vice Admiral and deputy chief of protocol. Cai helped to handle the heavy load of foreign affairs, an area in which Yuan was especially weak. In 1913, he held the post of director of the salt industry and tax bureau in the Ministry of Finance, playing a vital role in collecting tax revenue. In May that year, he and a friend contributed money to hold the first National Sports Meeting at the Temple of Heaven in Beijing; 96 athletes took part.

During World War One, he conducted diplomatic missions without the knowledge of the Foreign Ministry. One, in the autumn of 1915, was to find a way for China to enter the war on the Allied side; it wanted to be on the side of the victors at the end and reclaim the rights and privileges Germany had seized in the eastern province of Shandong. China offered to provide weapons and manpower; after 1916, 135,000 Chinese went to work in non-combat roles in France and Belgium. Beijing declared war on Germany, Austria and Turkey in August 1917.

But Cai's efforts were in vain. The Allies wanted the military, especially the naval, support of Japan, the predominant military power in Asia. They were not prepared to sacrifice this support in favour of China, despite its help for the war effort. After the end of hostilities, Cai and his colleagues saw the significance of this decision; in the *Versailles Peace Treaty*, China's demand for the return of the German possessions in Shandong was ignored and the victors awarded them to Japan.

Cai turns against his patron

Gradually Cai soured on Yuan, who had been his patron for the previous 20 years. Yuan had not accepted the idea of a democratic republic, preferring a feudal China in which he would be king (see chapter five). In 1915, Yuan revealed his plan to become Emperor, with the new dynasty to begin on January 1 the next year. Like the vast majority of Chinese, Cai was shocked and deeply disappointed. In addition, Yuan ordered the assassination of Dr. Sun Yat-sen, his chief political opponent and the president before him; Sun had fled to Japan for his personal safety. Yuan was also ready to accept the help of foreign countries to remain in power. Japan was willing to recognize him as Emperor but only if he accepted 21 demands it made on January 18, 1915; these were sweeping concessions to Japan in terms of territory and economic rights and the appointment of Japanese advisors to the Chinese government. When the demands became public, they provoked outrage. This forced Japan to remove eight of them; Yuan's government accepted the remaining 13 in a treaty signed on May 25. This was another reason for Cai to turn against his patron.

Yuan's reign as emperor was one of the shortest in China's history, lasting from January 1 to March 22 of 1916, when he gave up the position. Several provinces declared independence from his rule. Yuan died of uremia on June 5 that year, at the age of 56.

Cai shifted his loyalty to the new rulers, Li Yuan-hong and Duan Qi-rui. Both valued him as an able administrator with a wide knowledge of domestic and foreign affairs. After Yuan's death, he was appointed chief of the national tax bureau.

In July 1917, the military governor of Anhui proposed the restoration of Pu Yi. Cai refused to continue in his post under such a government, took leave and lived in the Six Countries Hotel (六國飯店) in the diplomatic area of Beijing. After the attempt to restore Pu Yi failed, Cai returned to his post. He carried out reforms to improve the tax system and increase national revenue. After 1918, Cai held the posts of chairman of a committee to modify tax regulations and principal of National Tax School. He received several medals from the Duan Qi-rui administration for his services to the government.

In March 1921, he chaired an international meeting on China's tariff autonomy in Shanghai. In November that year, he was one of three senior advisors to an international meeting in Washington on security and arms talks which also dealt with Chinese tariffs; it ended with a treaty signed by nine countries to convene a tariff revision commission and revise the rate of import duties to an effective five per cent. From 1923 to 1925, he was a member of a committee to regulate domestic and foreign debt. All this work was part of a long-term effort to reclaim China's sovereignty over its tariffs and finances; so much had been given away by the Qing Dynasty.

Cai also did diplomatic and charity work. In 1919, he was active in relief operations and, in 1925, was chairman of the Beijing Rotary Club (which he founded in 1924) and of the Society of Chinese Students in the U.S.. He was deputy chairman of the Chinese Red Cross. In 1922, he attended the wedding of former Emperor Pu Yi in Tianjin as a special guest. In 1925, the government sent him and two other representatives to Shanghai to deal with the aftermath of an incident in which police under British command killed nine demonstrators on May 30; they opened fire after a crowd of up to 2,000 tried to take over a police station where 15 ringleaders of a student protest were being held.

From June 1926, he was Minister of Foreign Affairs but resigned on October 1 because he believed he was unable to work effectively.

His final post was as chief of the tax bureau in 1927. He resigned from the job in May because of infighting between its British advisors, the banks and the government which was desperate for money to oppose the new administration set up by the Nationalist Party in Nanjing. At this point Cai retired from politics and went to live in the northeast port city of Dalian; he was 66. He kept contact with a wide range of people but avoided the Japanese, including the consul, who sought his company as one of the most eminent Chinese in the city. After the Japanese occupation of Manchuria in September 1931, he returned to live in Beijing.

Final years

Despite the heavy work schedule of his professional life, Cai continued to read widely in Chinese and English. In his retirement, he was in demand as a teacher and taught Chinese literature at Tsinghua and Yanjing Universities in Beijing. He also translated Chinese classics into English, including Tang poetry and the works of Lao Zi, one of China's most famous philosophers. His friends and colleagues gave him the nickname of "Scholar-General", in light of his military experience and literary prowess.

He wrote a book in English explaining the *Dao De Jing* (道德經), *The Way of Virtue*, the best known composition of Lao Zi. He also wrote *Chinese Poems in English Rhyme*, which was published by University of Chicago Press and well received internationally; this had 122 selected poems from the Tang period and included notes to the poems, an index of poets and chronological tables of the various dynasties. The foreword described it as the first translation of Chinese poetry into English by a native of China.

He died in Beijing on September 24, 1935, at the age of 75.

Cai Ting-gan.

The three Chinese representatives at the Washington Conference of 1921 - Liang Ru-hao (left), Madame Shi Zhao-qi (centre) and Cai Ting-gan (right).

Chapter Eight

唐寶鍔

1878 - 1953

Modernizer in Law

Tang Bao-er

Introduction

Tang Bao-er was the first Chinese to obtain a master's degree from a Japanese university. He became a Chinese diplomat in Japan, an interpreter for Chinese ministers and a co-author of a book on learning Japanese used by thousands of Chinese. He held senior positions in the Chinese government before and after the Xinhai Revolution, before becoming a lawyer and president of the Chinese Lawyers' Association. He wrote 20 books, on Meiji Japan, different aspects of Japanese laws and studies of the legal systems of different countries.

While most sons of Xiangshan learnt English as their first foreign language, Tang was sent to Japan. For 40 years following the Sino-Japanese War, Japan would be one of the most important countries from which Chinese students could learn the ways of the modern world and observe how it had successfully avoided becoming a colony of a European power, unlike many countries in Asia.

Between 1896 and 1937, 50,000 Chinese studied in Japan, including many of the country's most important figures of the 20th century – Lu Xun（魯迅）, Chiang Kai-shek, Li Da-zhao（李大釗）, Chen Du-xiu（陳獨秀）, Zhou En-lai（周恩來）, Qiu Jin（秋瑾）and Song Jiao-ren. It was closer and cheaper than studying in Europe or North America; the diet was similar and the language and culture familiar.

It was also a place of refuge for dissidents and exiles from the Qing government. Sun Yat-sen and Song Jiao-ren established the Tong Meng Hui in Tokyo in 1905. The predecessor of the Kuomintang, the Tong Meng Hui was a secret society and underground resistance movement formed by a merger of many Chinese revolutionary groups. Like the Chinese who went after him, Tang saw many things which he believed his country could emulate. He outlined them in the numerous books and articles he wrote.

Early life

Tang was born in 1878 in Shanghai of a family who came from Tangjiawan. He was the fourth of 13 children of Tang Zhao-hang (唐昭航), a prosperous tea merchant and a business associate of Tang Ting-shu. His was a wealthy family, unlike many of the other students who went abroad. In 1896, he returned to Tangjiawan and passed the Xiucai (秀才) exam and was accepted into the Foreign Ministry. A year earlier, China had been defeated by Japan and forced to sign the Treaty of Shimonoseki, under which it ceded Taiwan, the Penghu islands and the eastern parts of the Liaodong peninsula; it also recognized the complete independence of Korea, agreed to pay Japan a war indemnity of 200 million Kuping (庫平) taels (the Chinese treasury standard of tael, weighing 37.5 grams) and agreed to open four ports to Japanese trade. It was a treaty similar to those Beijing had signed with western powers after the First and Second Opium Wars.

The war and the treaty were a national trauma for China. Defeat by Britain, France and the other colonial powers had been humiliating enough for a country that considered itself the centre of the world. But to suffer a total defeat, by land and sea, at the hands of this small island was worse; for centuries, China had regarded Japan as a tributary state, which owed its language, culture and customs to its giant neighbour. Chinese often called its people "wo kou" (倭寇), meaning "dwarf pirates", a reference to their small stature and the fact that many Japanese pirates had attacked Chinese shipping in the 16th century. This insulting word is still widely used today by the mainland media and people.

The initial response of people to the defeat was anger and shame; this was followed by reflection and self-questioning. How could the Qing Empire be defeated by a country whose population was almost tenth of its size and had almost no natural resources? In 1894, Japan had 41.5 million people, against 388 million in China. Until 1868, the year of the Meiji Restoration, Japan had been similar to the Qing – a feudal system reliant on agriculture and fishing and closed to the outside world: foreigners were restricted to the single port of Nagasaki, as they had been restricted to Guangzhou before 1840 in China. In just 26 years, how could Japan have developed an army and navy strong enough to defeat China on its own territory and sign a treaty like a colonial power? What means had it used to modernize so rapidly? How had it learnt the military skills, industrial technology and economic organization of the west? What lessons could China learn from Japan? The countries had so much in common; so what Japan could do, China should be able to do and better.

This was the thinking of many reformists within the government. They believed that sending students to Japan was a quicker way to modernize China than sending them to Europe and the United States. This was a country similar in many ways to China; so it would be easier to adapt laws, regulations and customs from Japan than from the west. In addition, the Meiji government welcomed foreign students to its schools and universities; like the colonial powers of Europe and North America, it wanted to train foreigners in its language and ways of thinking and send them back to their home country with affection and personal ties to Japan which it could utilize later.

So, in 1896, just one year after the defeat, the Foreign Ministry sent 13 students from Tianjin, of whom Tang was the youngest, at 18; the oldest was 32. The Japanese Foreign Ministry organized a class for the students at a teachers' training college; they learnt Japanese, maths, physics and chemistry. They graduated in 1899, with Tang top of the class; he was only one of seven Chinese students still left. Four had left after just three weeks, because they could not eat Japanese food nor tolerate teasing by local students over their pigtails. In 1899, two others dropped out and returned home. In 1902, the place where Tang and his classmates studied became the Hong Wen College (宏文書院). Over the next 30 years, many famous Chinese would study there on their arrival in Japan, including Huang Xing (黃興), Chen Du-xiu and Lu Xun.

Tang stood out above the others by his mastery of Japanese. While it used many Chinese characters in its written form, it had developed two other alphabets as well as grammar and pronunciation completely different to Mandarin. Speaking it fluently required years of effort. Because of this fluency, Tang was sent to work as acting deputy consul at the consulate in Nagasaki in 1899; in 1901, he was promoted to the embassy in Tokyo. When the Qing government sent a delegation to Japan, he acted as their interpreter. He continued his studies at Waseda University（早稻田大學）and also worked as a teacher at Hong Wen College. When he graduated from the Department of Politics and Economy at Waseda in 1905, he became the first Chinese to earn a master's degree from a Japanese university.

In 1899, he put his language skills to use in co-authoring with another Chinese a book, *Rules of Japanese Language*（東語正規）, to help Chinese learn the language. It was published in 1900 by the Zuoxin Press（作新社）of Japan. It was republished several times and was popular with Chinese students. Professor Saneto Keishu（實藤惠秀）of Waseda University said that it was a landmark textbook for Chinese who studied the language, with sections on grammar, pronunciation, vocabulary and use of words. From 1896-1937, 50,000 Chinese studied in Japan and many used this book.

In 1905, Tang returned to China and was selected for the final imperial examination; he sat the test in the Hall of Preserved Harmony in Beijing. Two days later, he passed and was summoned to meet Dowager Empress Cixi Taihou and Emperor Guangxu; the latter issued a degree making him an A-Level Imperial Scholar, with the rank of Corrector in the Imperial Academy.

On December 21 that year, with the status of counsellor, he accompanied a member of the imperial family to Japan as interpreter. At mid-day on January 1, 1906, they met the Meiji emperor who invited them for a banquet; the Japanese side praised him for his high standard of interpretation. The next day, on the orders of the emperor, he received a medal of the fifth rank in recognition of this. On January 3, the team heard speeches from members of the cabinet on the Japanese constitution and reform of the financial system; Tang interpreted for them.

When the main party returned to China, Tang and eight others remained behind to do research. On his return to Beijing, Tang presented to the court a series of reports on Japan's reforms, including the judicial system, constitution, criminal law, railroad construction and education. He also translated information about Japan's police and government decrees, mining regulations, ore sand quarrying and notes on the railroad system. This reflected Tang's belief that China had much to learn from the Meiji reforms since 1868; Japan had succeeded in becoming a modern industrial and military power and retaining its imperial system. China imported from Japan new terms like democracy (民主主義) and revolution (革命) which had been invented there with Chinese characters. Similarly, the new Japanese word for hygiene (衛生) was imported; previously, this word had meant "preserving life".

Among the many Chinese who studied there was future president Chiang Kai-shek; he spent four years in Japan, first in a military academy and then serving in the Imperial Army from 1909 to 1911. Its severe discipline and exacting rules marked Chiang profoundly and influenced the way he lived for the rest of his life.

Tang and other Chinese who had studied in Japan drew this lesson: what Europeans had done, Asians could do just as well. What counted was not the race or the religion, but the system and the laws. China had land, mineral wealth and population larger than those of Japan. If it could modernize successfully, it could far eclipse its small neighbour.

After his return to China, Tang held many important positions.

Between 1906 and 1911, he was Principal of the Normal University and served in other posts under the Foreign Ministry, including deputy director, senior adviser to the Army and drawing up its criminal code. After the Xinhai revolution, the Qing court appointed him as counselor and secretary-general to Tang Shao-yi for the negotiations with the revolutionaries.

The change of regime did not affect his status; the new government was desperately short of people of his talent and experience. From 1911 to 1925, Tang worked as an advisor to the office of the provisional president and office of the Military Governor of Zhili; he was also senior adviser to the office of the governor of Suiyuan (綏遠) and he was a department chief in the police bureau of Guisui (歸綏). Suiyuan and Guisui are in Inner Mongolia and Guisui is now called Hohhot. Like other reformers, Tang fiercely opposed Yuan Shi-kai's attempt to restore the monarchy. On August 25, 1917, he went to Guangzhou to attend the extraordinary congress held by Sun Yat-sen and was elected a congressman.

He maintained his links with Japan. In 1920, he went there for a third time, leading a group of journalists. In 1922, he was a member of an official delegation that attended the Tokyo Peace Commemoration Exposition.

Like many sons of Xiangshan, he was bitterly disappointed by the leaders of the new republic; they were not building the modern state of which he and others had dreamt and were ignoring the advice of reformers like him. Two events in 1925 persuaded him to leave the government and concentrate on law (which he had studied in Japan) – the decision of the Beiyang government to dissolve the National Assembly and the death of Dr. Sun Yat-sen. (In the late Qing "Beiyang", meaning "northern ocean", referred to the three most important provinces of northern China – Hebei, Liaoning and Shandong)

After leaving government, Tang set up in private practice in

Tianjin, one of the cities with a foreign concession. He opened offices there and in Beijing and bought a large property in Simalu (四馬路) in Hebei, close to Tianjin; that became his principal residence. He excelled as a lawyer as he had done in government.

Tang was appointed legal advisor to the Beijing Railway Board. He represented the lawyers of Beijing and Tianjin at meetings of the Chinese Lawyers Association and was later chosen as a director and president of the association. With a Japanese partner, he set up the "Sino-Japanese Joint Legal Office". But, in 1939, his partner was ordered to return to Japan and the partnership came to an end.

Reflections

In July 1939, a Japanese law professor visited Tang in Tianjin. The professor was on a one-year mission to research relations between Chinese and Japanese culture, meeting Chinese who had studied in Japan and studying Chinese society. After he returned to Japan, the professor made a record of his meetings with Tang. They talked about how, before the war of 1894-95, the government had sent only a few people to study the Japanese language. After the war and especially after the Xinhai Revolution of 1911, the number increased rapidly to thousands. The returnees played an important role in the military, parliament and civil service of the new republic. Many of its laws were adopted from the Japanese example.

In his conversations with the professor, Tang criticized the attitude of Japan toward Chinese students. After they graduated, the universities did not care for them, unlike American colleges which organized reunions and paid attention to their graduates; "they strove to maintain the relations between the university and its alumni. It is very regrettable that the relations between the Japanese universities and their graduates are unlike that," Tang said.

For Tang, as for millions of other Chinese, the war with Japan was a tragedy. First, he lost his beloved property. After the outbreak of the war, he moved into the foreign concession of Tianjin for safety reasons, and left his former house empty. In spring 1939, a Japanese businessman moved into the house and turned it into a rubber factory. Tang did his best to get it back but failed. It was a big blow to him. After 1945, the house was auctioned as "enemy property" and bought by a member of a wealthy business family. His son, Tang Jia-zhuang (唐嘉裝) did his best to overturn the decision but failed. Tang was deeply disappointed and withdrew from the world; he stayed in his house in Tianjin.

Second, he saw the Japan he admired and sought to emulate taken over by military leaders intent on conquest and domination. They wreaked devastation on the land and people of China and other countries in Asia. The Japanese professor wrote that Tang did not express all that was in his heart; but he restrained himself when he talked of how the two countries joined by a common culture had become enemies. He had devoted his life to bringing the two together; now they were engaged in a terrible war. Who would want to read his learned books on Japan's constitution and legal system?

Legacy

Tang retired from the law in 1948 and died at his home in Tianjin in January 1953 of illness, at the age of 75.

He had made many contributions to Sino-Japanese culture. He left behind 20 books as well as other documents translated from other languages into Chinese, including those on the Meiji modernization of Japan. The books included his primer on learning Japanese and works on Japanese police and criminal law, its military law, its mining regulations and on comparative law of Japan, Britain, the U.S., Germany and France.

Old home

After he came back from Japan in 1905, Tang did not return to Tangjiawan. But his former residence there has been well preserved. It is in Shanfang Street and was built in the reign of the Emperor Tongzhi in the Qing dynasty. A two-storey building with a carved roof, painted gateway and granite-paved courtyard, it has a stone at the entrance which is engraved with designs of propitious animals, lucky clouds and the sun. There are eight pillars in the hall. The ground of the two floors is paved with red tiles. It has bedrooms, a study, a darkroom and a well.

Tang Bao-er.

Waseda University in Tokyo in 1911.

Chapter Nine

King of Tea

唐翹卿
1841 - 1925

Tang Qiao-qing

Introduction

Tang Qiao-qing is most famous for establishing the country's first tea export company and breaking the foreign monopoly of this most Chinese of commodities. Hua Cha (華茶 · Chinese Tea), the firm he founded, signed an agreement with Carter Macy, one of the United States' best known tea importers, and exported 80,000 crates in its best year, 1925. After the Opium Wars, foreign companies, mainly British, had dominated the export of tea and its sale around the world; Chinese firms did not have the knowledge of foreign markets nor the ships or finance to compete with them.

As a result, the foreign firms made a handsome profit from the product. Hua Cha fulfilled the dream of many Chinese – including other sons of Xiangshan involved in the tea business – and competed successfully with the likes of Jardine Matheson, Butterfield & Swire and Dent & Company. The brands which Hua Cha exported to the U.S. won a first prize at the Sesquicentennial International Exposition of 1926 in Philadelphia, a world fair to celebrate 150 years of America's independence from Britain.

Early life

Tang was born in 1841, the second of four sons of a poor rural family in Tangjiawan. Because his mother had given birth to many children, she died at an early age; his father had to raise the four boys on his own. Tang was only able to study for a few years before having to help his father work on the farm. Life was very hard.

His father decided that he would have a better future in Shanghai, where relatives and friends could help him find a career; so, when he was 14, he went on his own to China's largest and most prosperous city. There he met Tang Jing-xing (唐景星), a relative from Tangjiawan who was working in the customs bureau; he found a job for him in a tea company. Starting at the bottom Tang worked hard, studying the operations of the tea shops and accompanying his colleagues on purchase visits to tea-producing areas; he studied English. He learnt all aspects of the tea trade and earned the respect of his superiors. Tang Jing-xing introduced him to tea merchants and compradors of foreign trading firms. Tang later found a job as a comprador with a foreign company.

His knowledge and connections served him well and his income increased. Seeing the strong growth in demand and the opportunities this presented, Tang resigned his salaried post in 1867 and set up his own business, the Qian Shun An (謙順安) tea company in Jiujiang; he opened branches of it in Hankou and Shanghai. In 1868, with Tang Jing-xing and Xu Run , he set up the Shanghai Tea Company (上海茶葉公所); the three served as directors. He became one of the richest tea traders in Shanghai.

Production was concentrated in the south and east of China. Farmers sold their leaves to Chinese firms such as those owned by Tang or to compradors acting for the foreign companies. The terms of trade were biased against the farmer and in favour of the purchasers; for them, it was a lucrative business.

The money Tang earned enabled him to diversify into other sectors. He invested in the Renjihe Insurance Company, which by the time of the merger that created it in 1886 had a capital of one million taels. It had several major shareholders, including compradors of foreign banks. In 1883, Tang and two partners invested in the Chezhou (池州) coalmine in Anhui. In 1888, with two partners, including the father of Tang Bao-er, he invested in a real estate firm in Shanghai. He also invested in finance companies in Shanghai and Hong Kong with other people from Tangjiawan.

Competition from India

China's defeat in the two Opium Wars had brought radical changes to the tea industry. The opening of treaty ports led to a rush of foreign trading companies; by 1864, 68 of them had established offices in Shanghai, mainly British and American. One of their most important commodities was tea, especially black tea, which they exported from China to London, from where it was distributed to other markets. With the opening of the Suez Canal in 1869, the journey time to London was reduced from 127 to 58 days, cutting the price and making the business even more profitable. The habit of tea-drinking spread to the U.S., continental Europe and the Middle East. Considered healthier than cola or coffee, it became known as king of the world's three major drinks.

Before 1834, China had produced the vast majority of tea traded in the world, including that imported to Britain. Eager to end this dependence on a single source, the East India Company began to cultivate tea in the northeast Indian state of Assam; in 1839, the first auction of Assam tea took place in Britain. The British greatly expanded production in India and Ceylon, now Sri Lanka; by 1888, British tea imports from India for the first time surpassed those from China. Consumption in Britain soared; by 1901, it exceeded six pounds per person, compared to less than two pounds 50 years earlier. Tea – with milk and sugar added – had become part of the British way of life. During the two world wars, the government took over the import of this commodity because it judged the brew essential for the morale of the troops and the general public.

Foreign firms dominate exports

The wealth created by this explosion of global demand was largely in the pockets of the foreign firms who monopolized the export of tea. Chinese companies did not understand overseas markets, had no direct links with importers in those markets, were inexperienced in shipping and foreign exchange and did not have the qualified personnel they needed. They could not compete with their foreign rivals. Many Chinese entrepreneurs, including Tang Ting-shu, proposed that Chinese firms should export directly, to break the foreign monopoly and retain more of the high profit margin within China. But none could do it.

The breaking of the monopoly became the last great mission of Tang Qiao-qing's life.

In 1916, at the age of 75, he established the Hua Cha Company in Shanghai as China's first tea export firm. In association with other prominent tea traders, Tang raised 100,000 yuan in capital; he ran the firm with two of his sons, including Tang Ji-shan (唐季珊), his youngest son and 16th child. Tang had sent him as a boy to Britain, where he learnt English, received his education and studied the tea trade. Tang Ji-shan returned to Shanghai in 1916 and his father appointed him general manager of the new firm. The father merged his companies in Hankou and Jiujiang into Hua Cha and set up its headquarters at number 16, Museum Road in the city. It had branches in Hong Kong and the U.S..

In its first move into the export market, the company sold two brands of tea bags to San Francisco where it distributed them through Chinese-owned department stores; they were in bags of one pound, 0.5 pounds and 0.25 pounds. But Lipton dominated the market for black tea and Japanese brands the market for green tea. Without proper advertising and promotion, the two brands did not sell. After three years, the bags were broken and the broken tea sold for a bargain price. The company suffered a big loss and learnt a bitter lesson.

Undeterred, the Tangs invested a further 80,000 yuan in a new factory in the Zhabei district of Shanghai which they equipped with imported machines; they bought leaves directly from growers, to reduce costs to the middlemen. They launched two new brands Tian Tan (Altar of Heaven) and Chang Cheng (Great Wall) and secured long-term financial help from the Hong Kong and Shanghai Bank. Business improved. In 1923, they reorganized the firm into a shareholding company with an additional 100,000 yuan in capital; the Tang family held a stake of 80 per cent. They modernized the operations with new packaging and better quality and varieties. Despite his advanced age, Tang threw all his energy and fortune into the new venture.

To penetrate the U.S. market, the firm had to stop relying on Chinese companies there and join the mainstream. In 1924, it signed an agreement with Carter Macy, a large and well-established U.S. tea importer which had previously brought from British trading houses. Its best year was 1925, helped by a piece of bloodstained good fortune. On May 30 that year, Chinese and Sikh policemen under British command in Shanghai opened fire on a crowd of about 2,000 protestors, killing nine and injuring many, of whom 15 were sent to hospital. This was the same incident Cai Ting-gan was sent to deal with in its aftermath (see chapter seven).

The incident provoked a national uproar and a strike for three months by the city's dockworkers who refused to load cargoes on foreign-owned ships. This was a godsend to Hua Cha, whose shipments were not affected. It used wooden barges in Suzhou Creek to bring the crates to large vessels in the Yangtze River estuary. Carter Macy set up an office in Shanghai to establish the brands which it bought solely from Hua Cha; it helped with the promotion and marketing. In 1925, Hua Cha exported 80,000 crates, or 2,500 tonnes, of tea; it was the highest volume during the history of the company. It was during that year that Tang died of illness in Shanghai, aged 84. He had lived to see his dream fulfilled and the monopoly of the foreign firms broken.

Tang Ji-shan invested some of his earnings in the film industry and became a media celebrity. To promote his tea, he took Chinese film actress Zhang Zhi-yun (張織雲) with him to the U.S.. The company advertisements proclaimed him as the "Emperor of Chinese Tea" and Zhang as the "Empress of Chinese Tea". From May to November 1926, Philadelphia held a Sesquicentennial International Exposition, to celebrate 150 years of American independence. Hua Cha won a first prize for the tea it displayed at the Expo, together with porcelain from Jiangxi and silk from Jiangsu and Zhejiang.

In the 1930s, Hua Cha's exports averaged 60,000 crates or 1,900 tonnes a year, accounting for 10-18 per cent of tea exports from Shanghai and ranking the company the fourth largest in its field. This earned Tang Ji-shan the title of "The King of Tea".

Destruction

The Japanese invasion of China was a catastrophe for the company. In January 1932, its factory and warehouse in Zhabei were completely destroyed by Japanese bombing and artillery. The firm had sufficient goodwill from clients and banks to remain in business and find the money to rebuild its facilities. But the facilities were destroyed again during the Sino-Japanese battle of Shanghai in 1937. The Japanese took over the city.

After World War Two, the company re-opened in 1946 and exported a limited amount; but it was short of capital and equipment. Before 1949, Tang Ji-shan moved to Hong Kong and later to Taiwan. In 1950, the company's exports were only 169 tonnes. The company in the mainland was nationalized by the new government.

Family and charity

Tang Qiao-qing had 16 children, of whom seven died young. Of the nine who survived, four studied in the U.S.. One of the children served as Chinese consul in Luzon in the Philippines; he later worked with his father and younger brother as deputy general manager of the Hua Cha Company.

Tang Qiao-qing was active in public works. He founded an association for Guangdong people in Shanghai (上海廣肇公所) and, with Tang Ting-shu and Xu Run, aided the Renji hospital; he also funded the Gezhi College (格致書院) and Yinghua College (英華書院) in the city and gave financial help to poor, uneducated students. In Xiangshan, he founded schools, helped the poor and bought a small steamer which made regular journeys, carrying goods and passengers to and from the district to Hong Kong.

A tin of jasmine tea produced by the Hua Cha Company of Tang Qiao-qing.

Tang Ji-shan, the son of Tang Qiao-qing, and film actress Zhang Zhi-yun.

Chapter Ten

1864 - 1944

馬應彪

Retail Trailblazer

Ma Ying-biao

Introduction

In the 1930s, Shanghai was the commercial capital of China and one of the richest cities in Asia. Wealthy women, Chinese and foreign, went to shop, socialize and be entertained at four elegant department stores on Nanjing Road – Wing On (永安), Sincere (先施), Sun Sun (新新) and Da Xin (大新). All were set up by sons of Xiangshan born into modest families who had gone to Australia; there they made their first pot of money, returned home and went into business on a large scale. They are the fathers of China's modern retail industry.

Ma Ying-biao was one of these four remarkable individuals. He was born in December 1860 into a poor family in Shayong village, Xiangshan. While he was a baby, his father went to Australia to mine for gold. He had just three years of formal schooling before he had to go out to work to support his family. When he was 20, his father sent the money to buy passage on a boat for Australia. There he made his start in retailing, with a shop selling, fruit, vegetables, peanuts and Chinese products.

In 1892, he went to Hong Kong and set up business there. It would have been easier and simpler to remain in Sydney, where he would have had a comfortable and uneventful life. China was in a revolutionary ferment, the worst conditions for stable business. Ma decided to stay in China because he saw business opportunities and wanted to do something for his country; he joined the revolutionary party of Sun Yat-sen, a fellow son of Xiangshan. Sun told him that the rebirth of China needed business and enterprise. Ma decided to introduce the best business practices he had seen in Australia.

On January 8, 1900, Ma opened the Sincere store on 172 Queens Road, Central in Hong Kong; it was one of the earliest department stores in China. He went on to open more branches in Hong Kong, then Guangzhou, Shanghai and other cities in China and overseas - Singapore,

Osaka and London. He also opened a chain of hotels named East Asia (東亞). He expanded into a wide range of businesses, including manufacturing, banking and insurance; not all were successful. But they showed his entrepreneurial spirit and ambition to challenge the domination of foreign companies in China.

Ma was also active in charity. Having had only three years of schooling himself, he was keenly aware of the importance of education; he established evening classes, including literacy ones , for his employees. In 1915, he established a high school for girls in his home village and contributed to the building of others in Hong Kong, Guangzhou and Shanghai; he served on the boards of several schools. He donated a building to Zhongshan University (中山大學) in Guangzhou and was the first Chinese director of Lingnan University (嶺南大學). In 1920, he established the Lingnan Agricultural University, aided by money from the government; it trained specialists and developed better crops and seeds on an experimental farm. He was also active in relief work, delivering goods from his shops to victims of flooding in Guangdong. He was chairman of the Guangzhou Red Cross and served on the boards of hospitals in Guangzhou and Hong Kong.

This involvement was in part due to his religious beliefs; Ma was a devout Protestant and helped to set up the Young Men's Christian Association in Hong Kong. He lived modestly and employed only a few of his relatives, unusual for a Chinese family company at that time.

His final years were tragic. The Japanese occupied Shanghai, Guangzhou and Hong Kong and seized his businesses. In 1944, he had a stroke and died in Hong Kong on July 15, at the age of 84. Thirteen months later, Emperor Hirohito surrendered and the family was able to resume ownership and management of their businesses.

More than 110 years after its foundation, the Sincere Company lives on, with its headquarters in Hong Kong, where it operates six department stores and is listed on the main board of the stock exchange. Retail remains its core business; it has also diversified into property, securities trading, advertising, interior design, furniture manufacture and travel agency franchising, with operations in Taiwan, Britain, Australia and mainland China. Its annual revenue in the year that ended on February 28, 2012 was HK$498 million; members of the Ma family sit on the company board.

Early Life

Ma was born into the family of a poor farmer in Shayong village (沙湧村) in Xiangshan on December 21, 1860. His father, Ma Zai-ming (馬在明) was poor and could not find enough work to support his family. Like thousands of others, he wanted to join the gold rush in Australia but could not raise the money for the fare; so he borrowed and promised future wages to pay back. This was popularly known as "selling a piglet" (賣豬仔) – the workers were like animals that had been sold.

For the first 19 years of Ma's life, his father was absent, working in gold mines in New South Wales. The young man studied at a private school for three years but had to leave the classroom to support his mother, grandmother and other members of the family; he grew vegetables, fished and collected pig waste. It was a bitter, gruelling existence. In 1880, when he was 20, his father sent $200 – enough to buy his passage to Australia. He set sail, travelling on the bottom deck of the boat, as his father had two decades earlier; the voyage was very rough. They met on the quayside in Sydney; Ma had not seen his father since he was a baby.

He joined his father in the Victoria goldfields. There were miners from many nations – Germans, Italians, Poles, Americans, Irish, Scots and local people who had ventured out of the towns to try their luck; the Chinese were at the bottom of the heap and treated worse than the others, because of their language, dress, food and appearance. By the mid-1850s, there were about 17,000 Chinese; in teams, they worked the sites already mined and deserted by the Europeans. Like the white settlers, the government of Victoria did not welcome these new arrivals; it imposed an entry tax of 10 pounds on each Chinese immigrant arriving in Melbourne. The young Ma soon decided that there must be a better way to make a living.

Going into business

He went to work in a vegetable shop in Sydney run by an Englishman. But his English was very poor; it was only the whites who controlled the prices.

Improving English was a priority; he found an Irish woman who could speak Cantonese and needed help on her vegetable farm. He made an agreement with her: he worked on her farm in exchange for three meals and one hour of English instruction per day. So he studied intensively for three months and learnt the vocabulary needed for buying and selling vegetables. Then he opened his own vegetable stall; he wrote the correct names and prices of the produce. Each day his produce sold quickly; the stall-holders nearby asked him to help sell their vegetables.

The next step was to set up his own fruit and vegetable shop in 38 Mary Street, Sydney; he sold peanuts, bananas from Fiji and goods imported from China, in addition to local produce. Later, in 1890, he persuaded three partners from Xiangshan to invest in a larger shop in a better location selling fruit; he called it the Yong Sheng Company (永生公司). He opened other branches and started to import large quantities of specialty goods from China.

After 10 years in Sydney, he had established a good reputation among the Chinese residents of the city; one service they needed was a safe and reliable way to send money back to their families and pay for a bride in China. So he set up a money transfer company to provide this service, called Jin Shan Zhuang (金山莊).

He realized that, for the company to operate smoothly, it needed a branch in Hong Kong; in 1892, he went there to open this branch. The visit was a turning point in his life. He could have stayed in Australia; while anti-Chinese sentiment there was widespread, he had the acumen to run a good business and enjoy a comfortable life. If he had done that, the world would have never heard of Ma Ying-biao.

During his visit, two things changed his life. En route from Hong Kong to Guangzhou, he met Sun Yat-sen, a doctor trained in western medicine who was becoming the leader of the revolutionary forces opposing the Qing Dynasty. The two men knew each other but had not met for over 10 years. They had much in common: natives of Xiangshan and speaking the same dialect of Cantonese, they had gone to live abroad, learnt English, became Christian and understood the secrets of why the west was so far ahead of China.

Both were deeply unsatisfied with the Qing government and its failure to modernize and stand up to the colonial powers. Sun's greatest gift was his eloquence and persuasion. He told Ma that, for China to become a strong country, it needed a strong business sector and that entrepreneurs like Ma had an important role to play in national re-birth. "Business can save the nation," he said. Ma was moved and replied: "If there is anything you want me to do, just say it." It was his first realization that he could play a role in Sun's revolution.

The second realization came when he saw the business potential of Hong Kong. A British colony, it offered a higher degree of political and economic stability than the mainland. While British companies held the most important position, other firms were not excluded, provided that they followed the colony's laws and regulations.

So Ma decided to settle there; he managed his financial businesses and did foreign trade. Looking at the retail sector in Hong Kong and comparing with what he had seen in Australia, he saw a major opportunity. By the 1890s, its population had reached 300,000 and it had become a major trans-shipment port for the Far East. Customers in Hong Kong with a long shopping list had to go to many different outlets; most were small, crowded premises that sold only one type of product. Prices were not displayed; the customer had to bargain with the owner, who often did not show all his products; better items were hidden at the back for special clients, friends or those who would pay the most. The owner was in control and the customer the suppliant. It was a time-consuming and exhausting process; the customer often left believing that he had been cheated.

Ma believed that he could introduce into Hong Kong the business model he had seen in Sydney, especially David Jones, the city's oldest department store founded in 1838 on the corner of George Street and Barrack Lane. In David Jones, a shopper could find everything he or she wanted under one roof, with a variety in each product category. Prices were clearly marked and the goods were well laid out, with good lighting. The mission of David Jones, named for its founder, was to "sell the best and most exclusive goods" and carry "stock that embraces the everyday wants of mankind at large".

Jones chose a prime location and sold products to a wide clientele, both rich and poor. In 1887, he introduced Sydney's first hydraulic lift, to the astonishment of customers; in 1890, he released its first catalogue and began a mail order service.

Ma believed that many of these ideas could be introduced in a department store in Central, the business centre of Hong Kong, and that the city's population had sufficient spending power to make it profitable.

The first department store, Lane Crawford Co., had opened in 1850, founded by two British partners.

From 1896, Ma announced his intention to open Hong Kong's first Chinese-owned department store with fixed prices; he sought the advice and support of businessmen in the city. A majority opposed the idea, saying that such a store would not suit the customs and habits of Chinese; they would not provide financial backing.

But those who had been to Australia and the United States and seen western retail practices had a different opinion; they were willing to invest. Ma and 11 associates put up a total of HK$25,000. He told them: "Britain is a nation of commerce and commerce controls the national destiny. In America, business people have a high status in Congress and in the country, because they can do great things. Chinese traditional business people fight over trifles and cheat the customers who are not respected. We will set up a company, with fixed prices, a great department store. We will take back profits and power from the westerners, using business to save the country." So the new store was both a business decision and a statement of patriotism.

For the name of his company, he chose Sincere (先施), taken from a phrase in *Zhong Yong* (中庸), one of the classics of Confucianism. For him, the first principle of business was to establish a sense of trust and honesty with the customer. It would be the first Chinese-owned department store in the city, with 800 square feet and 40 staff. It would buy goods directly from manufacturers and offer prices below those in other retail stores.

The store opened on January 8, 1900 in 172 Queens Road Central with Ma as general manager. The crush of people was so great that the firm had to use a security company to keep order. It had three storeys, with a wide range of goods, staircases with mirrors and a system of fixed prices;

it issued receipts for purchases and customers could return goods if they were unsatisfied. The staff members had uniforms. Another innovation was female sales people. At that time, Chinese society was very conservative; foot-binding was widespread and a woman was supposed to remain at home, serving her parents, husband and family.

For most women, it was unimaginable that they could show themselves to hundreds of strangers for ten hours a day. Since so few women were willing to work as shop assistants, it fell to Ma's wife, Huo Qing-tang (霍慶堂), and her two sisters to take the lead. They went to the front of the store to greet customers. They inspired other women to follow their example. Huo was the first lady director of the firm.

Ma also introduced the practice of one day off a week. The new store took Hong Kong by storm; people from Kowloon crowded into boats to cross the harbour to see this new phenomenon. The crush was so heavy that the police had to keep order. Sincere caused a retail revolution. Other department stores followed suit; pretty sales ladies helped to promote business.

Ma was active in other sectors. In 1894, he opened in Hong Kong a company to help Chinese go abroad, get visas, buy boat tickets and move money abroad; he managed it for six years.

Beyond business, Ma was involved in the revolution of Sun Yat-sen. In 1895 he joined Sun's Xing Zhong Hui (興中會), the Revive China Society. He helped in propaganda and fund-raising, using the financial companies he had established. In 1905, he joined Sun's new organization, Tong Meng Hui.

In 1907, the Sincere Company paid its first dividend, with a profit of 90,000 silver dollars. Ma proposed a second store with four storeys in 215-221 Des Voeux Road Central, with 300 staff. Some shareholders opposed the idea, saying the investment was too large and that it would be hard to attract customers on such a broad street. His argument won the day and work began in 1907. This turned out to be a good investment.

He attracted customers with new items, such as a gift certificate which could be used to buy goods at Sincere shops for the same price as in any store in China; if a customer bought a large item he could not carry, the store would deliver it at no cost within 24 hours. It also had a counter with goods for only HK$1.

The company offered the staff lessons in English and abacus, as well as free cleaning of clothes, haircuts, medical care and cold drinks in summer. Many applied to work there.

On February 27, 1909, Ma registered the business in Hong Kong as a limited company, inviting seven Australian Chinese on to the board of directors and increasing the registered capital to HK$200,000. In 1911, he established an education department in Sincere, with classes to teach literacy. Competition in Hong Kong was heating up, with Wing On and Da Xin opening department stores in the city.

After the success of his operations in Hong Kong, Ma began to look at the big cities of the mainland, whose populations were substantially larger than that of Hong Kong. In 1910, he acquired a site of 4,000 square metres on the banks of the Pearl River in Guangzhou and started to build a five-storey department store. A military uprising in Guangzhou in April 1911 helped to precipitate the end of the Qing Dynasty. As a strong supporter of Sun Yat-sen and someone who had devoted time and resources to helping him, Ma was overjoyed.

On June 20, 1912, the new store in Guangzhou opened; it involved an investment of HK$400,000. In addition to the floors selling goods, it had a roof garden selling tea and beer, as well as barber shops, photographers, films and theatre. It also had a lift, which was a rarity in China. The new store took the city by storm and became very popular; by 1914, it had turned a profit. That year, he also opened in Guangzhou an East Asia Hotel which included lifts, restaurants and a billiard room.

The restless Ma was not content with his success in retail. He saw the fascination of his countrymen for foreign goods and how profits from them went to companies overseas. So he determined to go into manufacturing himself. In the early days of the Republic, he opened operations in Shanghai and Guangzhou, making textiles and daily necessities which supplied his own department stores as well as other customers. He opened 20 cosmetic factories across China, with the main plant in Hong Kong. In 1926, he registered there the Sincere Cosmetics Company, with a registered capital of HK$1.3 million. In the 1930s, the firm set up branches in Singapore and other cities in Southeast Asia. Cosmetics was the most successful of the product lines he went into. Others did not do so well and he was forced to close some factories.

In July 1915, he set up the Sincere Insurance Company of which he was chairman, with initial capital of HK$1.2 million. It did life, fire and property insurance and grew to have operations in more than 70 major cities of south, central, north and northeast China, as well as Singapore, Malaysia, Thailand and Vietnam. In November 1922, the Sincere Life Assurance Company started operations, with registered capital of HK$2 million, of which Sincere held 25 per cent and the rest was held by Ma's business partners and other shareholders. Business grew quickly, with branches opening in Shanghai, Tianjin, Guangzhou and Macao, Shiqi, Jiangmen and Shantou.

In 1913, he increased the capital of the Sincere firm to HK$800,000. He built a six-storey headquarters in Hong Kong, with three large entrance doors, lifts and a range of entertainments – restaurants and tea houses and dancing and magic performances in the evenings. It became the top entertainment centre in the Central district. In 1917, the registered capital reached HK$2 million.

A man of his ambitions had to open a flagship in the country's commercial capital – Shanghai. He decided on both a department store and a branch of his East Asia hotel. He prepared capital of HK$2 million and bought a site of 7,000 square metres on Nanjing Road, the city's most important commercial street. He spent three years on a steel and concrete building with eight storeys, which towered over the surrounding structures.

It was like the branch in Guangzhou but bigger and better – an up-market restaurant, cinema, dance hall and entertainment complex with magicians and opera performances. It had many firsts for Shanghai – a roof garden with potted plants, a tea shop, exhibition space, fixed prices, a wide variety of goods from home and abroad and lady sales staff.

Thousands of people crowded to attend the opening at 10a.m. on October 20, 1917, with fire crackers and ribbon-cutting. The lady staff were as much a hit as they had been in Hong Kong. The company put advertisements in newspapers; no-one applied. So Ma's wife herself started work on the cosmetics counter, together with a young woman who had been raised by a Christian minister. This broke the taboo and other ladies followed; they were very popular. By the second year, the revenue of the store exceeded the initial investment and overtook that of the Hong Kong branch. The company opened branches in Nanning, Harbin, Singapore, London and Japan.

By 1929, the capital of the Sincere Company had reached HK$10 million. His insurance and finance companies were flourishing too, able to compete with foreign firms in their sectors. Jin Shan Zhuang had branches in Singapore, Japan and the U.S.. The next major branch of the department store was in Macao; an eight-storey building, including a bank and a restaurant, opened on September 7, 1935 on 134-138 October 5

Street, on a site of 3.4 hectares. He also opened a branch of the East Asia hotel chain nearby.

The company continued to make firsts. It held a fashion show in Hong Kong, to show ladies' short trousers made of British fabric. It was even harder to find women to strut the catwalk than serve behind the cosmetic counter. They had to ask the ladies who waited on big gamblers at casinos to serve as models. It was the first such fashion show in Hong Kong history. By the 1930s, Sincere had become a multinational company based in Hong Kong. Department stores were its primary business, while it operated in other sectors in different countries around the world.

As a man with only three years of formal schooling, Ma was acutely aware of the importance of education and its role in building the nation. At the end of the Qing Dynasty, rates of functional literacy – not classical learning – were 30-to-45 per cent among men and 2-to-10 per cent among women.

Inspired in part by his Christian faith, he devoted time and money to education, both among his own staff and the wider society. He had published a 5,000-character textbook to help people learn to read. In 1915, he established the Light of the World Girls High School (世光女子高等學校) in Xiangshan, including vocational classes. In later life he became the director of schools and other educational institutions in Hong Kong and Guangdong.

He was the first Chinese director of Lingnan University, which had been established as a private university in Guangzhou in 1888 by a group of American missionaries. Initially known as Canton Christian College (格致書院), it was renamed Lingnan University in 1916 as it expanded into a university and the management passed into Chinese hands.

Ma funded the construction of several buildings, including one named after his wife, and proposed the establishment of Lingnan Agricultural University; this was approved and he became the chairman. The Guangdong provincial government gave 300,000 yuan in funds and, in subsequent years, an annual subsidy of 100,000 yuan as well as 900 mu (60 hectares) of land as an experimental farm. It set up departments for the cultivation of silkworms, farm technology and animal husbandry, to train specialists and develop better crops and seeds that were used across south China.

He was a director of Zhongshan University in Guangzhou; he and his wife each donated funds for a building, one of which now serves as a medical clinic. A statue of his wife stands at the entrance.

Ma was also active in relief work. As early as 1906, after severe flooding on the West River in Guangdong, he went there twice with his staff to deliver relief goods from the Sincere store. He did the same thing in 1915 and 1923, was chairman of the Guangzhou Red Cross and served on the boards of hospitals in Guangzhou and Hong Kong.

A devout Christian, in 1914, he established a Protestant cemetery at 119-125 Pokfulam Road in Hong Kong, overlooking the ocean and named it Ma He Nian Tang (馬合念堂). With fellow believers, he established the Young Men's Christian Association of Hong Kong and was its chairman in its second year.

At the end of the 1920s, Ma Ying-biao was at the height of his powers. In 1930, he turned 70. Despite his age, he was in excellent health, because of a modest lifestyle and calm temperament. He was one of best-known businessmen in Hong Kong and his fame had spread to Guangdong and Shanghai. The Sincere department store was a household name in China, with branches in Hong Kong, Guangzhou, Shanghai and other cities. The group also had the East Asia hotel chain and flourishing insurance and finance companies. In addition to running this large business empire, Ma was active in education, medicine and charity. He had more than fulfilled the mission given to him by Dr. Sun Yat-sen during their meeting more than 30 years before: "business can save the nation."

But, as with many Chinese, his life was devastated by the Japanese invasion. On January 28, 1932, the Japanese military launched an attack by air, sea and land on Shanghai, the start of a campaign that lasted until March 2. This short-lived conflict is known as the January 28 Incident. Ma lost his sixth son, Ma Shao-xiong (馬少雄), after he contracted a fatal infection when visiting injured soldiers in a military hospital in Shanghai.

In July 1937 Japan launched its all-out attack on China (hostilities known as the Second Sino-Japanese War), restricting the transport of foreign goods. This was a severe blow to the company, which imported many products from Europe and the U.S. and prided itself on giving customers a wide selection of goods. Ma was forced to purchase more from Japan, where he ordered goods with the same specifications; but, since Japanese products did not enjoy the same reputation as those from the U.S. and Europe, he did not advertise where they had been made.

On August 13, 1937, the main store in Shanghai was hit by Japanese bombs; his ninth son, Ma Shao-zong (馬少聰) was badly injured but survived.

In October 1938, the Japanese occupied Guangzhou, taking over the Sincere branch in the city. In December 1941, the invaders took over Hong Kong and his company. It was the worst nightmare for a man who had spent his life building a business from scratch: all his businesses were in enemy hands.

Remarkably, in 1943, he found the strength to escape from Hong Kong and cross enemy lines to reach the Nationalist capital in Chongqing. He returned by a similarly perilous route to the city in 1944. In July, he had a stroke and passed away on July 15 1944, at the age of 84. He is buried in the Protestant cemetery in Pokfulam which he had helped to establish 30 years before. Also buried there are other famous sons of Xiangshan, including Cai Chang, another giant of the retail industry.

After the Communist government took power in 1949, it took over Sincere's operations in the mainland, as it did other private companies.

Legacy

Ma Ying-biao died during the darkest hours for his family, his company and his country. But he left a great legacy, the more remarkable for a man born into extreme poverty who was able to attend school for only three years.

"My founding the Sincere Company has been to change the old ways of doing business in China," he said. "Living in Australia has opened my eyes to large-scale business organization and strategies. China will regain its national strength if Chinese businessmen modernize their practices to compete in international markets."

He was one of the fathers of China's modern retail industry, introducing management and practices that are widely followed today. His flagship store in Nanjing Road in Shanghai was followed by three rival retail giants – imitation being the sincerest form of flattery. His stores brought new and varied products and pleasure to thousands of customers; they offered restaurants, dance, film, theatre and tea gardens as well as dresses, shoes and cosmetics.

He and his wife made a great contribution to the women of China. During the late Qing, women were largely excluded from education, the work place and public life. The high-profile employment of women in his department store was a loud message to society – to give them an opportunity. He was also deeply involved in developing education for women, both at school level and as adults.

His deep involvement in education, healthcare and relief work showed that the pursuit of profit should not be the sole objective of an entrepreneur. Like the other sons of Xiangshan, he had seen for himself the wide gap between China and the western world and the need to work in many fields to bridge that gap. He was driven by both charity and patriotism.

An advertisement for the Sincere Company in Hong Kong promising a single price for each product.

The first Sincere Company, in the Central district of Hong Kong, in 1900.

The Sincere Department Store in the Yau Ma Tei district of Hong Kong.

The Sincere Department Store in Shanghai.

Chapter Eleven

蔡昌
1877 - 1953

*Department
Store Giant*
Cai Chang

Introduction

During the Republican period, China's four most famous department stores – Da Xin, Wing On, Sincere and Sun Sun – were all established by sons of Xiangshan. This is the story of Cai Chang, the founder of Da Xin; its Shanghai branch is now Shanghai Number One Department Store.

Poverty and Australia

Cai was born in Waisha village (外沙村) on November 3, 1877, the third of four children. His father was extremely poor and struggled to feed his family. The young man was able to study for only three years and had to drop out of school to help support his family; he worked as a farm labourer, herded cattle, fished at sea for crab and shrimp and even collected droppings (拾糞).

Like hundreds of other poor farmers in Guangdong, his eldest brother Cai Xing had gone to Australia to mine for gold. With another son of Xiangshan, Ma Ying-biao (see chapter ten), Cai Xing set up a fresh fruit stall in Sydney. In 1891, he came back to visit his family and took Cai Chang with him to Australia; the young man was 14.

On arrival in Sydney, Cai Chang worked as a helper in the general and fruit shops run by his elder brother and Ma Ying-biao. He helped his brother open a garden to grow fruit and vegetables in a Sydney suburb, to supply the shop. He also sent fruit to sell at a gold mine and exchanged it for gold. Soon he opened a small shop of his own in Sydney city, which sold general merchandise and fruit.

In 1899, Cai Xing moved to Hong Kong, taking the money which he had made and investing in the launch of the Sincere Department

Store (先施百貨公司), at the invitation of Ma. The capital of HK$25,000 came from him and 12 associates. The new store opened on January 8, 1900. Soon Cai Chang also went to Hong Kong, to work in the Sincere Company for Ma Ying-biao.

He had a good position and was well paid. But he was keen to start his own business. In his spare time, he studied culture and product management and visited foreign companies to see how they were run. He began with a small general store. In 1910, he made the decision to open a large department store selling goods from all over the world. Needing to raise money from others, he was strongly supported by his brother.

In 1912, the two brothers travelled around Guangzhou and Hong Kong to see merchants and seek funding; they raised HK$4 million and rented a small shop in Des Voeux Road Central, calling it Da Xin Department Store (大新百貨有限公司), with the sun as its logo. It opened in 1912. Its English name was The Sun. Competition was very fierce, with Sincere and Wing On nearby.

Cai Chang was manager. He got up every day at 4a.m. and attended to every detail of the business – quality of products, purchasing to ensure no fakes, fair and constant prices. He put good reputation above everything. Gradually business improved. During World War One, the foreign companies had no time to attend to the market in the Far East. It was an excellent opportunity to grow. Cai began to look to Guangzhou.

In 1916, the company set up a branch at Huiai Central Road, Guangzhou (惠愛中路,今中山五路). It sold general merchandise and also offered entertainment on the roof, with food and drink and bathrooms. It was a five-storey building of brick, wood and cement and employed 180 people.

In 1918, he opened another branch on the west bank (西堤) of the

Pearl River, a 12-storey iron and cement structure. The top three floors had balconies and open platforms: a car could reach the fourth floor by driving up a circular path. It had four elevators and its own power generators. It was considered one of the finest department stores in south China and attracted many visitors. Other features included restaurants with different cuisines and an entertainment garden on the roof, as well as a barber shop, camera studio and optician.

The two stores reduced prices during holidays and festivals. The annual turnover was 300,000–800,000 yuan. Da Xin did more business than its competitors in the city. Local people called the first shop "Da Xin inside the city" (城裡大新) and the second "Da Xin outside the city" (城外大新). Cai devoted most of his time to the Guangzhou company. The success of his businesses in Hong Kong and Guangzhou made him a well-known figure in the two cities.

His success in Guangzhou made Cai think of Shanghai, the biggest commercial centre in China so he conducted research and prepared carefully. After the Great Depression, the Nationalist government issued a law to encourage overseas Chinese to invest in China. Cai raised money in Hong Kong, Australia and Southeast Asia. In 1929, he raised HK$6 million, of which Guangzhou Da Xin held HK$1 million.

He was meticulous in choosing the site, personally standing at different spots on Nanjing Road which had a large volume of passenger traffic. He remained for several days on each one, from morning to night, with beans in his pockets, counting the number of passing people and vehicles. Finally, he chose the spot where Nanjing Road, Xizang Road and Laohe Road (勞合路，今六合路) intersect.

It was an area of different lanes (里弄), with the property rights held by many owners. To avoid the prices being driven up, he used agents to buy the sites separately. Finally, he succeeded in purchasing 8.2 mu (0.55

hectare) and hired a builder. The cost was 1.5 million yuan.

He then faced a complaint from the Ningbo Association in Shanghai (an organization of Ningbo people in the city), who said that the new structure would affect its building nearby. The two sides went to negotiations but to no avail. Finally they went to court. With the support of the Xiangshan Association and the Shanghai Mayor, Cai persuaded the concession authorities to accept his case and he won. He said that the new store would raise the tax revenue of the city and not affect the building; he won the lawsuit.

It took 13 months to complete the building, with 10 storeys and more than 17,000 square metres. It was the largest department store in the city, bigger than Sincere, Wing On and Sun Sun. It was modelled on the Daimaru Department Store in Osaka. The outside wall was covered by a milky yellow glazed tile, with a granite base. The building was designed to let in a maximum of natural light, with large windows. The inside was bright and airy, with both heating and air conditioning equipment. It had four entrances, six lifts, one of them exclusively for goods. In addition, there were two electric staircases bought from an American company, from the ground to the second and from the second to the fourth floor; they could carry 4,000 people per hour and reduced overcrowding.

It was the first department store in the Far East to use an electric staircase and many visitors who came just to see that, even if they did not shop. The first three floors were for selling goods; the fourth exhibited the works of famous painters and calligraphers and had offices for the staff; the fifth was a dance hall and restaurant to which Cai invited famous chefs to provide Chinese and foreign cuisine; from the sixth to the ninth there were cinemas, theatres, Beijing opera, magic and other amusements; and there was a roof garden on the top. Each day these facilities could entertain 20,000 people, to meet the demands of different classes of society.

Opening this store was a big risk. There were already three large department stores on Nanjing Road – Sincere, Wing On and Sun Sun – all opened by Xiangshan people between 1917 and 1926. They had nearly 20 years of history. Each had their own specialty. In addition, a war with Japan was threatening; and there was inflation in the economy.

Cai's decision to go ahead shows his bravery and sense of risk. In his favour were the scale, new equipment and new management. The automatic lifts were the first in Asia. The amusement facilities were very good, with 16 stages, including Beijing Opera, theatre, films, magicians and other programmes. Shanghai people liked new things. Sincere and Wing On had a high proportion of imported goods; Wing On's prices were higher. While it had foreign foods, Da Xin aimed more for the mass market; in the basement, it had cheap goods for the general public.

It opened on January 10, 1936, with Cai as president, brother Cai Hui-min (蔡惠民) as manager and eldest son Cai Nai-cheng (蔡乃誠) as vice manager. It had more than 800 staff, of whom a small number came from Hong Kong and Guangzhou; the vast majority were recruited through newspaper advertisements. There were many more applicants than places. Each had to pass an exam and be approved by Cai individually.

The company's principles were trust and sincerity. Customers should be warmly and politely received: they should be respected and given convenience in every way. Cai gave rewards and punishments. He required staff to take lessons after work, in arithmetic, abacus and English. Those who did well were given double salaries at the end of the year. He was very strict toward them, showing his pleasure and his anger. If they broke the rules of the store, he would tell them off immediately or punish their managers.

Before the opening day, the company advertised heavily in the major newspapers of Shanghai, offering the best goods from China and around the world. The ads boasted of its ten storeys, lifts that made access easy and heating and cooling systems that made every season like spring.

The store was very modern, with all staff members wearing uniform. Male staff wore black Zhongshan suits with black shoes; the department chiefs wore western suits with ties. The female employees wore long, rose-coloured Chinese dresses. Staff in the food and medical departments wore white uniforms. Each worker had a badge with a number. Cai borrowed heavily from the Chartered Bank to finance the project, using the building as collateral.

Ahead of the opening, he issued a statement in which he promised the best attention to the customers, loyalty and sincerity.

At seven on the morning of the opening, people began waiting and there was a large crowd by the opening at 10a.m.. The flow of people was unstoppable. At the opening, there were thousands of people on Nanjing Road and the crush was so large that they had to close four hours in advance, to clear up.

Business was good, reaching 3-to-4 million yuan a year between 1936 and 1939. It overtook the three other department stores in Shanghai. Cai had different accounts for the stores in Shanghai, Guangzhou and Hong Kong and treated each as a separate business unit, for profit and loss. He based himself in Shanghai, making inspection tours of the Guangzhou and Hong Kong companies several times a year.

Disaster of war

Like the owners of the other department stores, Cai was devastated by the war. After the Marco Polo Bridge attack near Beijing in July 1937, marking the start of the Second Sino-Japanese War, Guangzhou was repeatedly bombed by Japanese warplanes and the store on the west bank was seriously damaged. On October 20, 1938, when the city fell to the Japanese, the store was bombed and burnt by fire. It began just after 7p.m. on October 21 and lasted for four days and three nights. All the stock was burnt as the whole neighbourhood caught fire. Making matters worse, all the goods from the inner-city store had been moved there for safe keeping.

The Guangzhou firm was never able to recover from this blow. The west bank building became a skeleton and the site covered with rubble and overgrown with weeds. The two stores never re-opened after World War Two. Finally, in 1954, the west bank site became the Nanfang building and re-opened after 16 years as the Southern Department Store (南方大廈百貨商場). The Huiai site was renamed Zhongshan Number 5 Road Department Store. In 1987, the old building was demolished and a new one, the Xin Da Xin Department Store (新大新百貨大廈商場) was put up.

The Shanghai store was in the concession area and continued to operate; at that stage, the Japanese did not want to attack the foreign powers. After the battle for Shanghai began in August 1937, many residents moved into the concession for safety and business became even better. Its profits made up for the losses in Guangzhou. This enabled Cai to repay the large loan to Chartered Bank in 1940. After December 1941, the Japanese occupied the concession area and Hong Kong and took over the stores.

Return to Hong Kong

After the end of the war in August 1945, the Shanghai store had a brief period of prosperity. But, after 1948, American products were dumped in Shanghai and flooded the domestic market. The civil war caused the currency to depreciate. All the department stores in Shanghai were hit and Da Xin was badly affected, falling behind its rivals.

But the Hong Kong store was doing well so, in 1947, Cai brought the family to settle in Hong Kong and concentrated on the business there. He left the Shanghai business in the hands of his brother Cai Hui-min who deliberately ran it down by selling more goods and buying fewer and moving capital to Hong Kong. The reason for this was that, like other business people, they faced a high level of inflation and uncertainty about what would happen if the Communists took power.

In 1948, the Nationalist government imposed price controls and inflation worsened. This made Cai want to give up the Shanghai store even more. From 1946, the revenue of the Shanghai store fell below that of Wing On and Sun Sun. As the Shanghai store went downhill, the staff organized an "enterprise committee" to maintain its operations. In February 1950, he met a delegation of employees who asked him to return and run the business. He said he would consider it and sent HK$30,000 to the Shanghai store. But the Korean War broke out, the U.S. Seventh Fleet came into the Taiwan Straits and the situation became more tense. So he could not go back.

Passing

Cai's health was failing. In the summer of 1953, he died of illness in Hong Kong, aged 76. In November 1953, the Shanghai store was taken over by the government and became the Shanghai Number One Department Store.

Philanthropy

Cai Chang was active in charity work, as president of Tung Wah Number Three Hospital (東華三院), and gave money to social welfare causes in Shanghai, Guangzhou and Hong Kong. He was chairman of several hospitals in Hong Kong, including Tung Wah and Po Leung Guk (保良局). He was also active in the Hong Kong Zhongshan Relief Association.

In Guangzhou, a street was named Changxing Street (昌興街) in memory of the contributions of Cai Chang and his brother Cai Xing to the economy and culture of the city.

In the spring of 1929, he was chairman of the finance committee of the Zhongshan county government, after it was chosen as a model county under the leadership of Tang Shao-yi. He made many contributions to the county, to improve tax collection, enlarge the centre of Shiqi (石岐) (now a district of modern Zhongshan city), improve the building of roads and prepare for the opening of a bank.

In his hometown, Cai also donated money to the poor and in 1929 built a three-storey Lihe (禮和) primary school; it was later increased to six storeys. Children were admitted free of charge; the number reached 300-400. He invited excellent teachers from Hong Kong and Guangzhou and bore all the costs of the school himself. It remained open until the Sino-Japanese war. Now it is the Zhongshan Number 6 district administration office.

Cai's wife was a native of his local village named Liang (梁). She bore him two sons and two daughters. The first son, Cai Nai-cheng, studied in Britain and the second, Cai Wei-lin (蔡威林), studied in the U.S.. After they returned to China, they helped their father run the Da Xin company. Later the family lived in Hong Kong and abroad.

The Da Xin Department Store on Des Voeux Road in the Central District of Hong Kong.

An advertisement in a Shanghai newspaper for the opening of the Da Xin Department Store, on January 15, 1936.

China's first hand-held escalator installed in the Da Xin department store on Nanjing Road, Shanghai; this picture was taken in 1936, with Cai Chang standing on the lowest step of the escalator.

Chapter Twelve

郭樂
1874 - 1956

Shopping Tycoon

Guo Le

Introduction

The profile of Guo Le is remarkably similar to that of Ma Ying-biao and Cai Chang. He was born into a poor family and had limited formal education because he started work to help his family. In his teens, he moved to Australia, to join his brother. In Sydney, he started working in the fruit and vegetable business; he saved money and went into business on his own, first there and later in Hong Kong and the mainland.

Guo established his own brand, Wing On and diversified into textiles, insurance, banking, travel agencies and hotels. By the 1930s, it became the largest Chinese conglomerate in Hong Kong, with operations there, in mainland China and in Australia.

The family and their business were devastated by the Japanese attack on China; the invaders took over their operations. Guo moved to the United States in 1939 and set up the new branches of the Wing On company; it was there he died in 1956.

Like other private businesses, Wing On had its mainland stores nationalized after the Communists came to power in 1949. In April 2005, the Shanghai store resumed trading under the Wing On name but it belonged to a state-run firm. The exterior was restored to its pre-war appearance; the interior was drastically refurbished. Wing On is thriving today as a listed company in Hong Kong, with department stores as its principal business.

Ma, Guo and Cai were fathers of the modern retail industry in China. They introduced from the west modern management, accounting and recruitment methods and adapted them to the Chinese environment.

Early life

Guo Le was born in 1874 into a poor farming family in Zhuxiuyuan village, Xiangshan, one of nine children. As a young man, he joined his father working in the fields. When he was 17, he received permission to join his elder brother who had emigrated to Australia in 1883. He made the long voyage on his own and in 1891 joined his brother Guo Bing-hui who was working in Melbourne. But his brother died in 1892.

Guo Le moved to Sydney, where he worked for two years on a vegetable farm and then went to work in a fruit and vegetable shop jointly owned by a cousin (Guo Biao) and Ma Ying-biao. Over the next several years, he saved enough money to go into business on his own: he and four partners from Xiangshan paid 1,400 pounds to take over the Wing On fruit business (永安果欄) that had been set up by an overseas Chinese but fallen into difficulties. The new Wing On store opened for business in August 1897, with Guo as manager.

It began by selling fruit, Chinese goods and local items. Some of the fruit was Australian but most of it was from Fiji, which had abundant supply, good quality and low prices. The drawback was the travel time of one month by sailing boat to Sydney. To improve business, Guo joined the two major fruit companies in the Sydney market and opened a fruit company in Fiji. He brought four brothers from Xiangshan to help him run the business and sent one of them Guo Chuan (郭泉), to Fiji to run the operation there.

Guo was punctilious in paying his debts, which earned him a good reputation among Chinese and Australians alike. The fruit business grew from one shop to four and he set up a service to help Chinese to send remittances home. He bought a banana farm in Fiji, where he also set up a department store. As his business prospered, so he looked for new investment opportunities.

In 1900, Ma Ying-biao, his fellow son of Xiangshan, successfully opened the Sincere Department Store in Hong Kong. Guo, who was selling a wide range of goods in his Sydney store, decided to follow suit. He visited large department stores in Sydney and studied their method of operations. Then he, his brother Guo Quan and two partners from the Sydney company put up HK$160,000 and started the Wing On company in Hong Kong. He sent brother Guo Quan there as general manager.

On August 28, 1907, the Wing On company opened in 167 Queens Road, Hong Kong; it was a single room, with a staff of a dozen people. Its slogan was "a global department store"; it also offered services for overseas Chinese, such as remittances and advice on emigration and returning home.

The capital of HK$160,000 was insufficient for a large department store. Guo Quan was able to obtain personal guarantees from Ho Tung (何東) and other prominent businessmen; with them, he obtained loans of HK$2 million and HK$1 million respectively from the Hong Kong and Shanghai Bank and the Chartered Bank. In 1909, the company increased its capital to HK$600,000. Guo Le decided to move to Hong Kong himself to run the operations of the business there and in Sydney. He left the daily running of the fruit stores in Sydney to two of his other brothers. This was a turning point in his life. If he had stayed in Australia, he would have enjoyed a comfortable life. But he decided that opportunities at home were better. He could hardly have imagined how large the company would be 25 years later.

In 1912, the Guo brothers reorganized Wing On into a private company and the department store moved to a new site in Des Voeux Road, with four rooms and more than 60 employees. It aimed to provide everything a person needed – furniture, medicines, foreign liquor, tobacco, kitchen implements, clocks, clothes, cosmetics, suits, toys and sports goods. Its goods came from Europe, North America and China; each item had a fixed price. The store soon became one of the shopping centres of choice of the wealthy of Hong Kong. The Guos adopted a western-style form of operation, using as managers many overseas Chinese who had worked in North America or Australia; most of them bought shares in the company.

The brothers began to diversify. In 1916, they built a five-storey warehouse in Des Voeux Road, for the storage of western goods and canned food. In 1918, they built the Da Dong (大東) hotel on Connaught Road next to the waterfront. In 1919, they bought a textile factory to produce cotton goods. The company also invested heavily in real estate all over Hong Kong, buying more than 200 properties over several decades; thanks to the fast increase in real estate value over the last century in Hong Kong, this has proved a very sound investment and provided a strong capital base for the group today.

The brothers also expanded into finance. In 1915, they invested HK$610,000 in a property insurance company; it expanded its business to the main cities of China and in southeast Asia. In 1925, they set up a life insurance company and, in 1931, the Wing On Bank with capital of HK$2.2 million; it was registered in Hong Kong and Nanjing, then the national capital. With its headquarters in Hong Kong, it opened for business in 1934.

Like all Chinese entrepreneurs, the Guos turned their eyes to Shanghai, China's commercial and manufacturing capital. For Guo Le, Shanghai was essential for his business: "It is one of the four great cities of the world, the trans-shipment centre for our foreign trade and a place of competition between East and West. I have to be there."

In 1913, the brothers registered the Shanghai Wing On company with initial capital of HK$500,000. The First World War offered a golden opportunity to Chinese companies; the foreign firms that had dominated much of China's commerce were paralysed for the duration of the war. Their managers and staff were conscripted into the army, manufacturing was concentrated on military productions and transport links to Asia were severely disrupted.

The Guos increased the capital of their Shanghai firm to HK$2 million. They carefully considered the best site for a large department store before determining that it was on the southern end of Nanjing Road, "the number one commercial street in East Asia". The site was opposite that of the Sincere building.

Much of the real estate on both sides of the road was owned by Silas Aaron Hardoon, a Jewish entrepreneur who was the richest individual property owner in the city. Guo Quan drew up an agreement with Hardoon to rent nine mu (0.6 hectare) of land for 30 years. From April 1916, Wing On would build a six-storey commercial building with an annual rent of 50,000 taels of silver. After the end of the agreement, the building would pass to Hardoon; if he wished to continue renting it, Wing On would have the first option.

Construction of the department store began in 1916 and opened in September 5, 1918, on 635 Nanjing Road, opposite that of Sincere. In advertisements ahead of the opening, it promised more than 10,000 items, from Britain, the U.S., Japan and China, in 40 product sections over a floor area of 6,000 square metres. After the Sincere building, it was the largest department store in China. The flood of customers was so big that half of the stock for the first three months was sold out in 20 days. The firm used coloured slogans in the store: "Customers are always right." They could place an order for a product from another city in China; the purchasing department would endeavour to obtain it and have it sent by post. The store organized sales, lotteries and issued gift certificates and discount coupons (折子) in the form of post cards; these coupons became a popular gift among the wealthy of Shanghai.

Between 1918 and 1930, the Shanghai store made a total profit of HK$10.7 million, four times its initial investment and one of the highest rates of return for a Chinese company.

Guo appointed his younger brother Guo Kui (郭葵) as general manager of the new store; unfortunately, he died at a young age. Guo Le himself moves to Shanghai to be chief executive. They acquired a plot of 2.5 mu (0.16 hectare) next door and built a 22-storey commercial building, including restaurants and entertainment areas. On the fourth floor, they built two enclosed bridges between the two buildings, so that customers could enjoy a meal or recreation before or after their shopping. These were the first bridges of this kind in Shanghai. The new building was an insurance policy; if, after the expiry of the rental agreement in 1946, the Hardoon family demanded too high a rent, the company could move its department store in the adjacent building.

In December 1946, the agreement expired. Hardoon had died in 1931 and the ownership of the building had passed to his son George. He agreed to sell the site, which the Guo family acquired for US$1.125 million.

Diversification

The success of the department store and the wealth it generated persuaded the brothers to diversify. The firm expanded into insurance, warehouses, hotels, real estate and textiles, in which it became a major player.

The firm invested an initial HK$3 million in Shanghai Wing On Textile Company; overseas Chinese invested a further HK$3 million. It was a risky venture. China's technology in this field was far behind that of

Europe and North America; but the country had abundant raw materials and cheap labour.

By 1931, the firm operated 240,000 spindles in the city and created two well-known brands, Golden City and Great Eagle. Through expansion and acquisitions, it had by the mid-1930s become the second largest Chinese textile firm, with six factories and a full range of production, including dyeing and printing.

In 1916, Guo turned the firm into a public company that could accept outside investment, with a registered capital of HK$2 million. This continued to increase, reaching HK$6.3 million in 1931 and HK$8 million in 1942. During that time, the main store in Hong Kong increased from its original four rooms through acquisition of adjoining space, to reach 30 rooms on 40,000 square feet in 1931. Its main store in Central, Hong Kong occupies the same site today.

By the late 1930s, it had become the most diverse conglomerate in Hong Kong, with 15 subsidiaries in the group; with headquarters in the colony, it had operations in Australia and all over the mainland.

Ravaged by war

The Japanese attacks on Shanghai were a disaster for the firm. In 1932, their bombing destroyed two of its five textile mills; Guo and his brothers were devastated. They stopped their expansion. In 1937, the Japanese occupied the remaining three mills as well as the firm's dyeing plant. In 1937, Japanese planes bombed the Shanghai store and caused extensive damage.

In an attempt to protect their assets, the brothers set up an American company. Guo Le went to Hong Kong and then, in 1939, the

U.S., taking many of his managers with him. He left the mainland business to one of his brothers. He set up the Wing On company in San Francisco and New York and died in the U.S. in 1956.

Like other private businesses, Wing On had its mainland stores nationalized when the Communists came to power in 1949. In April 2005, the Shanghai store resumed trading under the Wing On name but it belonged to a state-run firm. The exterior was restored to its pre-war appearance; the interior was drastically refurbished. The rival Sincere department store returned to Nanjing Road in 1993.

Wing On is thriving today as a listed company in Hong Kong; department stores are its principal business. Wing On Company International reported a turnover in calendar 2012 of HK$1.868 billion, up from HK$1.764 billion in 2011, from revenue of the department stores and property rentals in Hong Kong, Australia and the U.S.. It operates five outlets in Hong Kong, with a total floor space of 360,000 square feet. Several members of the board of directors are members of the Guo family.

The founders of the Wing On company; second on the left in the front row is Guo Le and second on the right in the front row is Guo Quan.

The first Wing On store in Hong Kong at 167 Queens Road.

The Wing On store on Des Voeux Road in the Central District of Hong Kong.

The Wing On store in Shanghai.

Conclusion
The men who changed China

The 12 men described in this book were remarkable, because of what they achieved in their own lives and because they did so during a period of war, instability and dynastic change. They were models for Chinese to follow – and better examples than most public figures of their time. They changed China and moved the country forward on the long road of modernization. Unfortunately, they are largely unknown today; no history textbooks of the mainland, Taiwan or Hong Kong speak about them.

During the best part of a century from the birth of Yung Wing in 1828 to the opening of the Sincere and Wing On department stores in Shanghai, the vast majority of Chinese lived and worked in the same village and the same community. Our 12 were also born into such a rural community but lived in the great cities of Beijing, Shanghai, Guangzhou and Hong Kong and travelled abroad, a privilege reserved for a tiny fraction of the population. It was this that gave them knowledge, experience and insights unavailable to their fellow citizens. They brought this knowledge back to China and used it to help the country.

How should we measure their success?

In material terms, those who went into business were the most successful. Tang Ting-shu and Xu Run established many companies, gave employment to thousands of people and earned enormous wealth for themselves. Two of these companies – China Merchants Group and the Kailuan Group – live on today as large and influential conglomerates in shipping, transportation and coal. But we should measure their success less in the wealth they created than the example they set as Chinese entrepreneurs.

It was the Europeans – primarily the British – who had created the industrial and trading city of Shanghai and made it the economic centre of China. They established its modern banks, trading firms and shipping companies; it was they who had the links to the markets abroad which imported Chinese tea, silk and porcelain and exported opium and manufactured goods. For them, the Chinese were the "natives", like people of British colonies around the world, useful in procuring the raw materials they needed and arranging the sale of their imports; but it was the foreigners who controlled the process and earned most of the profit.

With the backing of Li Hong-zhang and the Self-Strengthening Movement, Tang and Xu set up companies that were able to challenge this foreign monopoly and stand on their own feet. They used modern management and accounting methods and hired the most-qualified staff, foreign and Chinese; they took business risks to advance the cause of the company. They were a lesson to their peers that they could compete with the powerful foreign conglomerates. In 1877, China Merchants bought one of its competitors, the American firm Russell & Co., for 2.2 million silver taels. It was the first purchase of a foreign shipping company by a Chinese firm. Tang and Xu were models of how to be a Chinese entrepreneur.

Huang Kuan was also a model. An orphan, he left China at the age of 18 and spent nine years abroad, in the United States and Scotland, the last seven without the company of other Chinese students. Then he returned to China and devoted the rest of his life to the care of patients, Chinese and foreign, in Hong Kong and Guangzhou.

The first Chinese to graduate from a western medical institution, Huang mastered a difficult and complex discipline in a foreign language and he put the knowledge to practical use for the benefit of thousands of ordinary people. Although offered a comfortable government post, with more pay and less work, he resigned after less than six months because he could not endure the culture and living style of the civil servants. Huang preferred to return to his hospital in Guangzhou with its long hours and heavy patient load. He was also a pioneer in transmitting what he had learnt, translating many texts into Chinese and establishing, with his American partner, a medical school. So he was a model of a doctor dedicated to his patients, offering them services which 30 years before had been unknown and unavailable to China. And he was a model of compassion in devoting himself to their service rather than to the accumulation of money.

For those involved in politics – Yung Wing, Tang Shao-yi, Cai Ting-gan and Tang Bao-er – the picture is more confused. All four were knowledgeable, well qualified and clear on what they wanted to achieve. But they were players in a political environment that was chaotic, vicious and complicated; it was the end of the Qing Dynasty and the opening years of a new republic dominated by military leaders, warlords and factions fighting for power. Government was person-centred; as the Chinese saying goes, "When a man becomes a high official, even his chickens and dogs go to heaven". Or, conversely, when the man loses his black official's hat, what happens to his chickens and dogs? Policies and posts were often hostage to the career of a single leader; if he fell from office, so did those he had appointed.

Yung Wing suffered most from this. After graduating from Yale University, he had the opportunity to settle in the U.S. possessing the knowledge and connections to have a good life there. But he was loyal to his country and determined to make it better. He did not realize how hard it would be. On returning in 1855 he found the government fighting the Taiping Rebellion in one of the biggest wars of the 19th century. In Zeng Guo-fan, Li Hong-zhang and other members of the Self-Strengthening Movement he encountered kindred spirits who wanted to reform China as he envisaged.

The Jiangnan shipyard he helped to build in Shanghai in 1865 became the largest arms factory in East Asia; it produced steel and steam boats. In 2009, it moved to a new site in Changxing Island, where it is manufacturing China's first domestic aircraft carriers.

Yung's greatest achievement was to bring modern education to

China. The reformers approved his plan to take students to the U.S. and the time spent implementing it constituted the happiest years of his life. But in 1881, after only 11 years, conservatives at the court torpedoed the plan and ordered all the students home; only three had completed university.

For the rest of his life, Yung proposed many reforms to the government; but none was accepted, except during the short-lived 100 days of reform in 1898. Then the Empress Dowager ordered the arrest of the emperor and the execution of the reformers. Yung had to flee for his life.

He was a man ahead of his time; many of his ideas were implemented by later governments. So, perhaps, his greatest achievement was himself – a Chinese patriot who put aside personal advantage for the national good and strove to introduce the best elements of the west into China and make it a better country.

Tang Shao-yi played a vital role in the North-South negotiations that followed the Xinhai Revolution of October 1911; he helped to ensure that there was no civil war and no regicide and that the emperor stepped down in favour of a civilian president.

But he was, like the others, a victim of his nation's politics. In a normal country, he would have made an excellent Foreign Minister or ambassador to Washington, London or Tokyo. But China was anything but normal. Tang's skills were not well utilized and he left the central government in disgust in 1920, returning to his hometown in Xiangshan.

The seven years he spent there as county chief, from 1929 to 1936, were the most productive of his life; he was, at last, master of his own house and able to implement the reforms that his county needed. But even that, in a small rural county far from the centre of power, could not last. A warlord from Guangzhou jealous of his success and popularity drove him out with his soldiers. Having lost hope, Tang went to live in his house in the French concession of Shanghai.

Both Cai Ting-gan and Tang Bao-er gave their best efforts to the service of the country. During his 26 years in the government, Cai made important contributions to the military, tax and finance, customs and diplomacy. Like Tang Shao-yi, he would have made an excellent Foreign Minister or Minister of Finance. Tang Bao-er's specialties were law and Japan. A modern legal system was an essential building block of the new republic; through his writing, his advocacy and his practice, he argued for China to adopt better laws and a sounder legal system. But its politics were not stable nor its leaders wise, and his advice largely fell on deaf ears.

The same could be said of Tang Guo-an, who was, with Yung Wing, the strongest moral advocate among the 12. Throughout his life, he campaigned for the causes he believed in – against opium, foot-binding of women, inequality between foreigners and Chinese, corruption in the government and business, and the low standard of public hygiene. In doing so, he antagonized powerful interests in society.

He was, like Yung Wing, determined to bring modern education to China. His greatest achievements were the return of Chinese students to the U.S., of which he took charge, and the establishment of Tsinghua University. Although he was its president for less than three years before his untimely death, Tang laid the foundation for what has been ever since one of the most important educational institutions in China; many political, academic and business leaders have studied there, in the Nationalist as in the Communist period.

Tang Guo-an and Yung Wing were moral leaders; probably that is their greatest legacy. Both had the skills and contacts to migrate to the U.S. or Europe and enjoy a comfortable life there; but they declined. They chose instead to devote their energies to reform and improve their motherland, even though they knew the political and social environment was largely hostile to their ideas. Yuan Shi-kai stole the money that Tang needed for Tsinghua University; Yung had to flee for his life after the failure of the 100 days of reform in 1898. They left behind them the model of someone who put moral conviction and the good of their country above money and material benefit.

The achievements of the three fathers of China's modern retail industry – Ma Ying-biao, Guo Le and Cai Chang – are easier to measure. They established flourishing department stores in Hong Kong, Shanghai, Guangzhou and other cities, introducing a quality of management and service and a variety of products that Chinese had never seen before. For his part, Tang Qiao-qing established the country's first tea export company and broke the foreign monopoly of this key commodity. He was a pioneer whom many other Chinese would follow.

The stores of the three retail kings provided goods, entertainment, dining and shopping pleasure to millions of people. Visit the department stores and shopping malls in cities across China and you can see their legacy. Their businesses were devastated by the Japanese invasion, the civil war and nationalization by the new government after 1949. But the ideas they planted lived on. This spirit of commerce and entrepreneurship was one of the secrets of China's success in the post-1978 reform and open-door period. Other Communist states, like North Korea and the former members of the Soviet Union, were unable to produce a sufficient quantity of consumer and light industrial goods, even after they abandoned Socialism. How different it was in China. Once Deng Xiaoping opened the door to private business and foreign investment, the spirit of Ma, Guo and Cai came quickly back to life; entrepreneurs like them came from the mainland, Hong Kong, Taiwan and the diaspora to set up factories and shops. In just 25 years, China became the light industrial factory of the world. It was also significant that Deng chose Guangdong – the home of the 12 – as the first province for his reforms; it has the longest history of private entrepreneurship in China and the best access to the wealth, experience and contacts of the Chinese diaspora.

Another theme of the book is as relevant today as it was in a century ago – China's interaction with the west, especially the U.S.. In the past 30 years, tens of thousands of students from the mainland, Taiwan and Hong Kong have followed the footsteps of Yung Wing, Tang Guo-an and the others to study in the U.S.. They have gone for the same reasons – to learn advanced arts, science, technology and other knowledge not available at home, improve their mastery of English and have the experience of living in an advanced country. When they graduate, they face the same question as Yung Wing – stay there or return home; for many, it is not an easy decision.

In the nearly two centuries since Yung graduated, the situation of Chinese in the U.S. has improved dramatically. At that time, the vast majority worked in mines, construction sites and railroads, ran restaurants and laundries and earned the lowest wages. They were on the margin of society, often compelled to stay in areas designated for them and not allowed to live among the whites. Their status mirrored that of the country they came from: looked down on and victims of discrimination. This left many with a strong sense of inferiority. In 1882, the U.S. government passed the Chinese Exclusion Act, banning all immigration of Chinese labour; it was not repealed until December 1943. Yung, Tang Shao-yi, Tang Guo-an and the others who studied there were exceptional; they received privileged treatment, studying at the best schools and universities and mixing with the country's elite. As a result, they felt no sense of inferiority toward whites and regarded them as equals, no better nor worse than Chinese.

So, when they returned from their studies, they had a big shock – they found themselves second-class citizens in their own country. While their teachers, classmates and host families in the U.S. had treated them with respect and dignity, most westerners they met in China looked down on them, despite their good education and excellent English. This was a reality they found hard to accept, as were the unequal treaties which their government had signed. How could they be equal citizens in the U.S. and second-class ones at home?

The close connection with the U.S. continued through the Nationalist period. The government which took power in 1927 was deeply involved with the U.S.. Song Mei-ling（宋美齡）, wife of President Chiang Kai-shek, was more American than Chinese. "The only Oriental thing about me is my face." she said on her return to Shanghai in 1918, after studying for 10 years in the U.S. including at the elite Wellesley College. Many senior officials studied in the west, especially the U.S., and had relatives and assets there. U.S. support, military, material and diplomatic, was critical to China during World War Two.

This link with the mainland was broken after 1949. When the Communists took power and joined the Northern side in the Korean War, China and the west became enemies. But Taiwan continued to engage with the west and sent thousands of students there, especially the U.S., for the same reasons as the mission of Yung Wing and Tang Guo-an. Many faculty of Tsinghua fled to Taiwan where they established a new campus at Hsinchu; the Boxer Indemnity money paid for more than 1,000 students from there to study in the U.S.. The university was especially strong in science and technology and played an important role in the growth of the island's economy. Once China had established diplomatic relations with the U.S. in 1979, students from Tsinghua in Beijing resumed the journey of their predecessors and crossed the Pacific for graduate studies; so have hundreds of thousands of others from campuses across the country.

In the early years, the vast majority of students from Taiwan stayed in the U.S. because of better job opportunities, few openings at home and fears of political instability. Of the 16,825 who went from Taiwan between 1960 and 1969, only 561 returned. The Nationalist government accepted this loss of talent; it did not have the career openings for such well-qualified people and did not want idle graduates who might become dissidents. After the end of martial law in 1987 and the maturity of the island's economy, more Taiwan students returned after graduation in the U.S.; they had more choice of work and felt more optimistic about its future, thanks to greater civil and political liberties.

A similar pattern has occurred since Chinese students started to go to the U.S. in 1978. Initially, the vast majority stayed there; in 1990, President George Bush Senior granted permanent resident status to nearly 50,000 after the military crackdown in Beijing a year before. But the smooth transition of power after the death of Deng Xiao-ping, average annual growth rates of eight percent, better jobs, higher pay and a more pluralistic society have persuaded an increasing number to return. The government has adopted policies to entice them, such as preferential housing and new R & D facilities for returning Ph.Ds. First, they were called "haigui" (海歸) – a pun on sea turtles who swim home to lay eggs and in this context meaning those who returned and easily found work. Now many are called "haidai" (海帶) – kelp, meaning that they have no work because there are too many of them.

According to figures from the American Institute of International Education and the State Department, more than 800,000 international students studied at U.S. universities in the 2012 academic year. Chinese ranked first with 235,000, ahead of South Korea and India. For Chinese, the U.S. remains the first choice for overseas study, ahead of Australia, Japan, Britain and Canada. From 1978 until the end of 2012, more than 2.6 million Chinese studied abroad, making China the world's top source of overseas students, according to the Xinhua news agency. Chinese parents are prepared to make enormous sacrifices to fund their child's study abroad, especially the U.S., even if it means going into debt.

Students are ambivalent about the U.S.. They are patriotic and criticize U.S. militarism and aggression overseas; many agree with the government view that Washington's long-term strategy is to work with Japan, South Korea and countries in Southeast Asia "to contain China" and prevent it becoming a global power. If a Chinese plays an American at Wimbledon, they passionately want the Chinese to win.

But they love U.S. films, music, style and freedoms. Many students who go to study there plan not to return. One student told me: "My parents told me it would be better not to return. If that means marrying an American, they are fine with that. Then they would move to the U.S. to join me." Marrying an American is the quickest way to obtain the right to reside there and later U.S. citizenship. Another student was in the opposite situation: "My parents are willing to fund everything, including study and living costs, on condition I do not marry an American and promise to return to China."

Whether they stay depends on many factors. If they are graduates of science or technology, they may find in the U.S. career prospects, laboratory facilities and funding not available at home. Some find a job that is temporary; it turns into a permanent one and their employer applies for a visa for them. Or they fall in love with an American lady. But emigration comes at a cost. They leave behind their family, friends and networks at home; they lose the lifestyle, cuisine, magazines, television programmes and culture they enjoyed at home. Their children are unlikely to read and write Chinese; their grandchildren certainly will not. Since the mid-1990s, the proportion of those returning has increased: the Chinese economy has grown strongly, offering many opportunities, just as the growth of the U.S. economy has slowed and the living standard of many in the middle class – to which Chinese migrants are likely to belong – has deteriorated.

If they return home, they can participate in one of the most exciting periods in China's history and be in the mainstream. If Yung

Wing had stayed in the U.S., we would not have heard of him; it was only by going home that he could make the contribution he did. The same is true of many Chinese who have set up IT and high-tech companies at home after studying in the U.S.. One good example is Robin Li (李彦宏), who studied at the University at Buffalo and came back to China to co-found search engine Baidu（百度）. In March 2013, he was ranked as the second richest man in China with a net worth of US\$ 6.9 billion. Could he have had the same success if he had stayed in the U.S.?

The status of Chinese in the U.S. has grown immeasurably since the days of Yung Wing and Tang Guo-an, thanks to the success of Chinese immigrants there in many fields and the fact that China is now the world's second biggest economic power. As their country has advanced, so Chinese, especially educated ones, feel equal with Americans, just like the 12 in this book.

They changed China and played an important role in its modernization; it has been a long journey, one that is still in progress. We hope that their biographies will interest the reader and, perhaps, inspire him or her to follow their example.

Editor   Donal Scully

Designer Hoi Yee Man

First Published in October 2014

Published by Joint Publishing (H.K.) Co., Ltd.
20/F., North Point Industrial Building, 499 King's Road, North Point, Hong Kong

Printed by C & C Offset Printing Co., Ltd.
14/F., 36 Ting Lai Road, Tai Po, N.T., Hong Kong

Distributed by SUP Publishing Logistic (HK) Ltd.
3/F., 36 Ting Lai Road, Tai Po, N.T., Hong Kong

Copyright © 2014 Joint Publishing (H.K.) Co., Ltd.

ISBN 978 - 962 - 04 - 3665 - 9